Animal
Liberation

ANIMAL LIBERATION

A Graphic Guide

Text by
Lori Gruen & Peter Singer

Illustrations by
David Hine

Camden Press

The illustrator, editor and authors would like to
thank Anna Borzello, whose enthusiasm caused this
book to be commissioned, Hilly Beavan and Anthony
Lawrence of *The Animals Diary*, Helen Fox, Philip
Churchward and Robert Sharpe of the BUAV, and
Peter Hine, for their generous and invaluable help.

Published in 1987 by
Camden Press Ltd
43 Camden Passage, London N1 8EB, England.

Text © Lori Gruen & Peter Singer
Illustrations © David Hine
Designed by Sue Lacey

Set in 10 on 12pt Century Schoolbook
by Impeccable Photosetting, London.
Printed and bound by
Richard Clay Ltd, Bungay, Suffolk.

British Library Cataloguing in Publication Data

Gruen, Lori
Animal Liberation: a graphic guide. – (graphic guides)
1. Animals, Treatment of
I. Title   II. Singer, Peter. 1946 –
179'.3   HV4708
ISBN 0-948491-21-3

Contents

CHAPTER ONE

The Animal Liberation Movement

For more than a year they had done everything they could to find out what was going on in the laboratory. Nobody would talk to them. Now they felt there was only one thing left...

28 MAY 1984 EARLY MORNING... FIVE MASKED FIGURES DESCEND INTO THE BASEMENT OF THE UNIVERSITY OF PENNSYLVANIA MEDICAL SCHOOL...

THE RAIDERS CREEP THROUGH THE BUILDING UNTIL THEY REACH THE LABORATORY OF DR. THOMAS GENNARELLI.

THEY SEARCH THROUGH THE CLUTTER UNTIL THEY FIND WHAT THEY HAVE COME FOR ...
THIRTY FOUR VIDEO TAPES THAT WILL SHOCK THE WORLD!

Thomas Gennarelli's Head Injury Laboratory had first caught the attention of Animal Rights activists in March 1983 when the *Toronto Globe and Mail* ran a story on his experiments with baboons ...

Brunt of research borne by monkeys

By PAUL PALANGO

A group of monkeys in a Philadelphia laboratory is finding out what it is like to be in a prizefight... the monkeys are being whacked on the head by a machine, knocked out and sometimes cut open to find out what kind of brain damage can be caused by blows of a certain force.

> WE'RE TRYING TO KEEP OURSELVES OUT OF THE NEWSPAPERS

Gennarelli himself had been evasive. But they did learn that cruelty in animal research crosses national boundaries. After suffering the blows, monkeys' brains were being sent to Scotland's Glasgow University for analysis.

12

Now, as a result of the actions of the five masked members of the underground Animal Liberation Front, everyone was about to learn just what Gennarelli had been doing to the animals in his laboratory.

The ALF knew that Gennarelli and his collaborators videotaped their gruesome experiments, apparently to provide a record of what happened during and after the injuries they inflicted; but there had been absolutely no way of knowing just how awful the situation really was for the animals.

After leaving the laboratory, the raiders went to a safe place to view the tapes. What they saw horrified them ...

- conscious, unanaesthetised baboons struggled as they were being strapped to an operating table where their heads would be accelerated and de-accelerated very rapidly in order to inflict severe brain damage.

- animals writhed in pain as experimenters performed surgery on their exposed brains.
- hammers and screwdrivers were used to remove the helmets into which the animals' heads had been cemented before the experiment.

- experimenters smoked while operating on the animals.
- experimenters dropped surgical tools on the floor and then picked them up and placed them back into an animal's brain, without cleaning them.
- experimenters mocked and laughed at frightened, suffering animals.

As they watched the videotapes, the ALF members knew that if what they were seeing could reach the general public, it would shatter forever the illusion that all animal experimentation is done by dedicated scientists who care for their animals and do not allow them to suffer. But the ALF could not make the tapes public without exposing their members to prosecution. So they gave copies of the tapes to People for the Ethical Treatment of Animals (PETA), a Washington, DC, animal rights group.

15

● The battle

Upon receiving the tapes, PETA attempted to negotiate with the University of Pennsylvania. Their requests for a meeting to discuss the tapes were acknowledged only by a form-letter reply.

After waiting a month and realising that the University was going to try to cover up, the Animal Liberation Front struck again. This time the raiders targeted the University of Pennsylvania Veterinary School, which had publicly defended Gennarelli's head injury experiments.

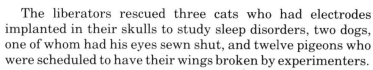

The liberators rescued three cats who had electrodes implanted in their skulls to study sleep disorders, two dogs, one of whom had his eyes sewn shut, and twelve pigeons who were scheduled to have their wings broken by experimenters.

Meanwhile Alex Pacheco, Chairperson of People for the Ethical Treatment of Animals (PETA), was busy editing the 60 hours of video tapes. He finally managed to cut them down to a 30-minute version which he ironically titled *Unnecessary Fuss*, after Gennarelli's comment that he didn't want publicity which would 'stir up all sorts of unnecessary fuss among those who are sensitive to those types of things'.

Armed with *Unnecessary Fuss*, PETA representatives scheduled a showing on Capitol Hill, to show Congress how $1 million of public funds were being spent per year at the University of Pennsylvania. The showing was cancelled by government officials. Determined nevertheless to publicise the abuse of animals in this federally funded laboratory, Pacheco and other PETA members went to Philadelphia to hold a news conference. They showed the tape, and excerpts from it were subsequently seen on national television, provoking widespread shock and revulsion.

But not everyone believed that what the ALF had done was right. After the tape was shown, several activists were served with subpoenas by the Philadelphia District Attorney's office and ordered to testify before the Grand Jury about the ALF break-ins. Determined to 'break the back of the animal rights movement', the Philadelphia DA's office began putting on pressure. Animal rights activists were harassed, their telephone and credit card records were seized, and their work was disrupted. Law enforcement officials tried desperately to catch the raiders while completely ignoring the hideous crimes being carried out in the Head Injury laboratory.

Shortly after the raid, an inspector working for the United States Department of Agriculture (which has responsibility for enforcing the law relating to laboratory animals) reported on Gennarelli's laboratory:

[The lab] did not comply with the minimum requirements of the Animal Welfare Act ... cages and rooms need 100% better sanitation ... the primate cages do not meet space requirements ... ventilation appears to be very poor ... there is a build-up of urine and debris on walls and floors in all rooms ... cockroaches everywhere you look ... (USDA report, June 1984.)

People everywhere – even scientists and vets – began speaking out against the experiments:

After carefully reviewing the videotapes, I have reached the conclusion that the researchers depicted in the tapes were among the most unprofessional and insensitive individuals I have ever seen in my years of scientific work.
(Dr Ned Buyukmihci, Veterinary Ophthalmologist.)

I cannot imagine that anyone could observe this sequence of events and still contend that these experiments could have any experimental validity ... the methods shown on the videotapes make it clear that the animals were subjected to unnecessary pain, that the experimental protocols followed in the work invalidate the results and that perhaps of most concern, nowhere in the original grant is there anything other than casual lip service given to the value of this work towards treating human disease.
(Doctor Jay Glass, Neurophysiologist.)

In many of the scenes, the animals seem to be treated with unnecessary cruelty and in other scenes the plight of the seriously injured animals seems to be a matter of amusement and disrespect on the part of the investigators. We found the film deeply disturbing not only because of the basic moral and legal issues that are raised, but also because there is some question as to whether the research conforms to accepted norms of scientific procedure.
(Thirteen law professors, University of Pennsylvania School of Law.)

19

A video tape has been circulating which provides shocking and disturbing information about some of the procedures followed at the Clinic in its research using primates ... on the basis of the evidence provided by this film, it is obvious that the quality of the research being done at the ... clinic ... is open to very serious question on scientific grounds. It is absolutely clear that federal funding of such research is inappropriate and provides information of dubious scientific value.
(Sixteen Members of the US Congress, Letter to HHS Secretary.)

In April 1985, almost one year after the break-in, the experiments were still going on. Fifteen hundred animal

rights activists from all over the country marched at the University to protest about the painful experiments and the administration's lack of concern. Despite increased pressure from animal rights groups, concerned citizens and the US Congress, university administrators and National Institutes of Health (NIH) officials repeatedly praised the laboratory. The Director of NIH, James Wyngaarden, who was the chairman of the Department of Medicine at the University of Pennsylvania for three years, said the laboratory 'was one of the best in the country'.

The frustration grew when activists learned that the NIH had given the Gennarelli laboratory one of the highest ratings possible and that the laboratory's funding would continue.

● The sit-in

To highlight the continuing NIH funding of the experiments, PETA began preparing a peaceful sit-in at NIH headquarters in Bethesda, Maryland. On July 15, 1985, over 100 people from as far away as California and Maine, Washington and Florida, entered NIH administration building, and in shifts, made their way up to the 8th floor. The activists converged on the office of the Director of the National Institute for Neurological and Communicative Disorders and Stroke, which directly supported the head injury experiments. There they vowed to remain until the experiments were stopped.

To the surprise of the protesters – who had been prepared for arrest and a night in jail – the NIH did not use force to evict them. Instead NIH attempted to play a waiting game, hoping that when night fell the protesters would get tired and go home. It didn't happen. Instead the protesters expanded their territory and took over the entire wing.

On the second day NIH officials cut off the telephone service and would not allow any food or supplies into the building. That did not intimidate the activists, who found a box and some rope and lowered it from a window, down eight storeys, where it was filled with food, toothbrushes, clean shirts, banners, a television (to watch the news coverage), a bullhorn, and other necessities. That night dozens of supporters gathered to hold a candle-light vigil and the activists on the inside sang and chanted with their supporters on the outside.

By the third day, the tenacious campaigners were getting worried but they held their ground and kept their spirits up (despite NIH'S attempt to freeze them out by putting the air-conditioning on high). People did their laundry and hung it out the windows to dry amidst the banners. Everyone wondered what would happen next.

Around 11.00 am on the 4th day, a PETA spokes-person from the outside ended the suspense by joyfully announcing that the Secretary of Health and Human Services had stopped Gennarelli's experiments. The exhausted protesters had accomplished what they had set out to accomplish, an end to the pain that the innocent baboons were forced to endure at the Head Injury lab. The year-long battle was over.

● Another victory

The victory was soon followed by another: only a month later, the federal government banned all animal experiments at the misnamed 'City of Hope' research facility. This California experimentation centre had been the target of another ALF raid. In December 1984, West Coast liberators rescued over 100 animals from what they called an 'animal concentration camp'. The ALF found sick and dying dogs left in cold, damp cement runs. Cats were forced to lie in their own excrement.

Many animals were emaciated and unable to move. Paint was peeling off of the walls, tiles were coming up off the floor, and cages were rusted and broken. Autopsy reports removed from the facility revealed that several animals bled to death, some died after 'routine injections', many perished due to surgical incompetence, and two animals died of 'overcrowding' and 'bite wounds'. As many as half of the dogs scheduled to be used in one cancer study died before the experiment even began.

With two major victories in a brief space of time, and the increased momentum of direct action campaigning, the ALF has made sure that no experimenters are safe from public scrutiny. The animal liberation movement has rocked the scientific establishment, and made its mark on the US public and government.

● Who are the ALF?

Members of the Animal Liberation Front are activists who directly intervene to stop animal suffering. At the risk of losing their own freedom, ALF members:

1. liberate individual animals and provide them with permanent, loving homes;
2. obtain documentation of animal abuse, which is not otherwise available;
3. damage and destroy property used in animal exploitation.

As part of their personal campaign against animal abuse, ALF activists do not eat animal flesh, and many of them use no animal products at all. They come from all social classes, age groups, professions, races, religious and political persuasions, and all are prepared to go to jail, if that is what it takes to end animal suffering. They serve as the community's conscience by revealing the horrors that are inflicted on animals behind closed doors. They are committed to doing all that it takes to end animal abuse, short of harming any living being.

Direct action for animals began in England in the early 1960s when a group called the Hunt Saboteurs Association was formed. Hunt 'sabs' physically disrupt hunts by laying false scents, blowing hunting horns to send hounds off in the wrong direction, and chasing animals away to safety. The Hunt Saboteurs have effectively ended many traditional hunting events all over England.

In 1972 a group of Hunt Saboteurs decided that more militant action on behalf of animals was necessary and thus

25

the Band of Mercy began. The Band of Mercy, named after a group of animal rights campaigners in the nineteenth century, smashed guns used on bird hunts and sabotaged hunters' vehicles by slashing tyres and breaking windows. The group also began fighting other forms of animal abuse, setting fire to pharmaceutical laboratories and burning boats used for hunting seals.

In 1975 two members of the Band of Mercy, Ronnie Lee and Cliff Goodman, were caught trying to break into a laboratory and were sent to prison. After the arrest, support for direct action grew, and in 1976 the Animal Liberation Front was set up. Since that time, thousands of animals have been rescued and millions of pounds worth of damage has been caused. It has been reported that ALF actions occur daily in Britain, ranging from raids on research laboratories to smashing the

windows of fur shops. Today there are animal liberation groups in Britain, USA, Australia, Italy, France, Germany, Canada, and New Zealand. While there are no formal communications between the groups, they all share the same goal: to save animals from suffering here and now.

One ALF member put it this way:

> I see participating in ALF's raids not as a momentary forfeiture of the highest human values – goodness, generosity, and the like – but rather as an embodiment of them ... We feel a sense of urgency for the animals whose pain and imminent death is absolutely real to them today.

● The formula for success

ALF actions have been important, but they are just one of many components that add to the success of the growing animal liberation movement. Like previous movements for social change, the animal liberation movement is made up of a wide range of groups whose activities complement each other.

Paving the way for animal liberation, young, activist organisations, such as People of the Ethical Treatment of Animals (PETA) and the Fund for Animals (in the United States), the British Union for the Abolition of Vivisection (BUAV), ARK II in Canada, and the Australian group Animal Liberation, have taken to the streets to protest against animal abuse. PETA, one of the fastest growing grassroots organisations, was instrumental in bringing about the first arrest of an animal experimenter for cruelty to animals. They also spearheaded a campaign that closed a

military wound laboratory, where live animals were to be shot with high velocity weapons. In addition to playing a central role in exposing Gennarelli's Head Injury lab and the City of Hope, PETA was responsible for closing down the largest horse slaughter operation in North America. The Fund for Animals, headed by the outspoken Cleveland Amory, has orchestrated many daring rescue missions. They air-lifted wild donkeys out from the Grand Canyon before they were to be shot, hand-carried deer from the Florida Everglades before hunting season was to begin, and prevented the shooting of wild goats on California's San Clemente Islands.

The British Union for the Abolition of Vivisection played a similar role to PETA in relation to a raid by the South Eastern Animal Liberation League on the Royal College of Surgeons' experimentation centre. The BUAV publicised photographs of monkeys used in the experiments, one of whom had 'CRAP' tattooed across his forehead. Using evidence obtained as a result of the raid, BUAV prosecuted the Royal College of Surgeons, one of the most respected medical organisations in the world. The prosecution resulted in a conviction at the first trial. Although this was subsequently overturned on appeal,

the publicity surrounding the trial convinced many people that all is not well in animal experimentation in Britain.

Political lobbying organisations also serve a valuable role in the promotion of animal rights. The National Alliance for Animal Legislation was a moving force in bringing the Gennarelli Head Injury Laboratory to the attention of Congress. The Society for Animal Protective Legislation was instrumental in strengthening the Animal Welfare Act in the United States. In Australia, the Australian and New Zealand Federation of Animal Societies lobbied successfully for a Senate Inquiry into Animal Welfare, which has demonstrated abuses in the live export of sheep from Australia to the Middle East and has recommended against the keeping of dolphins in captivity.

Whether it's Artists for Animals or the Animal Legal Defense Fund, the Farm Animal Reform Movement or Buddhists Concerned for Animals, every group has contributed to the increased awareness of unnecessary animal suffering.

If it weren't for the organised letter writing campaigns, the thorough research, the lobbying, the boycotts, the protests, the break-ins and, above all, the deep resolve that the oppression of animals by human beings cannot be allowed to continue, the Head Injury Laboratory would not have been shut down, animal experiments would not have been banned at City of Hope, new legislative restrictions on animal exploitation would not have been enacted, and calls for animal liberation would not fill the air.

CHAPTER TWO

The Animal Liberation idea

THE HINDU 'Laws of Manu'
He who injures harmless beings from a wish to give
himself pleasure, never finds happiness, neither living
nor dead. Having well considered ... the cruelty of
fettering and slaying living beings, let him entirely
abstain from eating flesh.

A JAIN MAXIM
Harmlessness is the only religion.

FROM THE BUDDHIST SCRIPTURE 'Dhammapada'
Because he has pity on every living creature, therefore
is a man called 'holy'.

PLUTARCH FROM THE 'Moral Essays'
Other meat-eaters you call savage and ferocious – lions
and tigers and serpents – And yet for them murder is
the only means of sustenance! Whereas for you it is
superfluous luxury and crime!

A Jain wearing a mask to prevent the accidental swallowing of mosquitoes.

● The roots

Concern for animal suffering is not new. Developed around 1500 BC, the most ancient of all works of philosophy and religion, the Indian *Vedas*, denounce meat-eating because of the injury and death it brings to animals. The religion of the Jains, which dates from about 500 BC, teaches that non-violence is a guide to all of morality. Jains are often ridiculed by Westerners for the care they take to avoid injuring insects or other living things while walking or drinking; but they also looked after sick and injured animals thousands of years before animal shelters were thought of in Europe.

34

Buddhism is another example of an ethical system which takes animals seriously. The compassion of the Buddha, who lived from 563-483 BC, extended to all sentient creatures, and even today the first Buddhist vow is to abstain from taking life - a principle which extends to animal life.

At one time, such ideas were also held by Western philosophers. Pythagoras, the Greek thinker born in 570 BC, was a vegetarian, and the first century philosopher Plutarch wrote a moving essay against the cruelty involved in eating animals; but for the most part the Western religions – Judaism, Christianity and Islam – have taken a different view.

● The western tradition

In *Genesis* we read:

And God said, Let us make man in our own image, after our likeness: and let them have dominion over the fish of the sea, and over the fowl of the air, and over every living thing that moveth upon the earth.

For many centuries, the orthodox interpretation of Christianity accepted this idea of our dominion over animals, and intensified the difference between us and them by the importance it gave to the idea of an immortal soul – something which only human beings were said to have. Once Christianity became the official religion of the Roman Empire, views like those of Plutarch dropped out of sight. Animals were seen essentially as our property; that is, as *things* for us to use.

There have been occasional exceptions. The Old Testament book of *Isaiah* contains a lovely vision of a utopia:

The wolf and the lamb shall feed together
and the lion shall eat straw like cattle.
They shall not hurt or destroy in all my holy mountain.
(LXV, v.25)

And immediately afterwards there is a condemnation of animal sacrifices, which are said to be 'loathsome practices' not to the Lord's liking. In the book of *Proverbs* we read: 'A righteous man cares for his beast, but a wicked man is cruel at heart'. Among Christians, in the fourth century both St Basil and St John Chrysostom spoke out in favour of kind and gentle treatment to animals, who, St John Chrysostom said, 'are of the same origin as ourselves'. In medieval times St Francis of Assisi became famous for preaching to the birds, and he has since become a symbol of concern for animals.

Tragically for animals, a different interpretation of the Christian message gained the upper hand. Christianity spent its formative years in the shadow of the Roman Empire, which revealed its attitude to animals in its gladiatorial contests. In these 'games' Caligula had four hundred bears slaughtered in a single day; Nero made four hundred tigers fight with bulls and elephants; and when Titus dedicated the Colosseum, five thousand animals died in the celebration. The modern bull-fight is the direct descendant of these cruel spectacles.

No wonder, then, that the Christian thinkers who were most influential during the long centuries of Christian domination of European thought either ignored animals, or said that what happened to animals did not really matter. 'Does God care for oxen?' St Paul asked scornfully, obviously believing that the answer must be 'No'. St Augustine, one of the most influential of the early 'Church Fathers', explained the New Testament story of the Gadarene swine (in which Jesus is described as casting devils out of people by sending them into a herd of pigs who are made to drown themselves in the sea) by saying that Jesus was teaching us that we have no duties towards animals. This view was accepted by the dominant figure in Christian theology of the middle ages, the thirteenth century scholastic Saint Thomas Aquinas. He wrote that nothing we do to animals can be a sin – unless of course they are our neighbour's *property*, in which case harming the animals would be a sin against our neighbour.

The philosophy of Aquinas became the official view of the Roman Catholic Church. As a result, as late as the middle of the nineteenth century, Pope Pius IX refused permission for the founding of a Society for the Prevention of Cruelty to Animals in Rome, on the grounds that to grant permission would have implied that human beings have *duties* to the lower creatures. The position of the Roman Catholic Church at that time was as stated by the Jesuit priest, Joseph Rickaby:

> We have then no duties of charity, nor duties of any kind, to the lower animals, as neither to sticks and stones ... Brutes are as *things* in our regard ...

● The Anti-cruelty movement

The first serious efforts to stop cruelty were made by the Puritans, in the seventeenth century. At that time, bear-baiting was a popular pastime. This 'sport' involved chaining a bear to a stake, and then releasing packs of dogs to attack her. It has been said that the Puritans opposed this practice

'not because it gave pain to the bear, but because it gave pleasure to the spectators'; but this is unfair. The Puritans did regard bear-baiting as a profanation of the sabbath, but at least some of them saw animals as creatures of God, to be loved as we love God. Indeed, the Puritans who went to America and founded the Massachusetts Bay Colony can be credited with the first law against 'Crueltie towards any bruite creature which are usuallie kept for man's use', enacted in 1641.

In England, which has a reputation for being dotty about animals, the first efforts to make laws to protect animals were made only 180 years ago. They were greeted with laughter and scorn, and the first attempt was defeated. The Society for

The Prevention of Cruelty to Animals was founded in 1823 by some of the same people who were leading the campaign against the slave trade. For its time, the society was a very radical organisation indeed.

The idea that we should protect animals from cruelty achieved respectability when Queen Victoria gave it her support, and the Society for the Prevention of Cruelty to Animals became 'Royal'. But at the same time the organisation became more conservative. It worked hard against the most blatant kinds of cruelty, especially to animals like dogs, cats and horses, but it didn't challenge the much greater systematic cruelty which occurs all the time in the raising of animals for food, and the use of animals in experiments.

'The Queen hears and reads with horror of the sufferings which the brute creation often undergo from the thoughtlessness of the ignorant, and she fears also from experiments in the pursuit of science. The Queen feels it to be a sort of reproach that even in a single instance they should occur within her dominion.'

(Queen Victoria, Letter to Lord Harrowby, 19 June 1874.)

The growth of animal experimentation gave another boost to the movement for animal welfare because of the horrific –though entirely accurate – details that emerged about what was being done to animals. Claude Bernard, a pioneer of vivisection in France, himself said:

> **A physiologist is no ordinary man. He is a learned man, a man possessed and absorbed by a scientific idea. He does not hear the animal's cry of pain. He is blind to the blood that flows. He sees nothing but his idea.**

Bernard's wife was apparently unable to stop her ears and eyes in this way, especially when her husband began mutilating dogs in their kitchen. She and her daughter began a French animal welfare society.

Yet the nineteenth century anti-cruelty movement was built on the assumption that the welfare of non-human animals deserves protection *only* when *our* interests are not at stake. Animals were thought of as 'lower creatures'. Human beings were seen as quite distinct from, and infinitely superior to, all forms of animal life. If our interests conflict with theirs, it is always their interests which have to give way.

● Rights for animals

The new animal liberation movement has dared to question the assumption that *human* interests must always prevail. Animal liberationists want to extend the basic moral ideas of equality and rights – which, at least in theory, most people now regard as applying to all *human* beings – to animals as well.

At first this appears crazy. Obviously animals cannot have equal rights to vote, say, or to free speech. But the kind of equality which animal liberationists wish to extend to animals is a special kind: *equal consideration of interests*. And the basic right that animals should have is the right to equal consideration.

This sounds like a difficult idea, but it is really quite simple. It means that if an animal feels pain, the pain matters as much as it does when a human feels pain – if the pain hurts just as much. *Pain is pain*, whatever the species of being that experiences it.

Suppose that you slap a horse across the rump with your open hand. The horse may feel something, but because of the nature of his skin he presumably feels little pain. Now imagine giving a naked baby a similar blow. The baby would feel much more pain. Therefore, if there is nothing more to be said about the slaps – no special justification for giving them – it is worse to give the slap to the baby than to the horse. But there must be some kind of blow, perhaps with a whip, which would cause the horse approximately the same amount of pain that the slap inflicts on the baby. Then – still assuming that there is no special reason for inflicting either blow – the principle of equal consideration of interests tells us that it would be just as wrong to hit the horse as it would be to hit the baby. The fact that the baby is human, and the horse is not, makes no difference to the wrongness of inflicting the pain.

Of course, with both humans and animals there are circumstances in which it is justifiable to inflict pain. Sometimes we do it for the good of the one on whom we inflict the pain – as when we lance a boil, or apply a stinging disinfectant to a wound. Sometimes it can even be justifiable to inflict some kinds of distress on one person, or animal, for the greater benefit of others. Here we must be much more careful; but taxing one person so that others can have the necessities of life is widely, and we think quite properly, regarded as acceptable. A similar 'trade-off' of interests may

be justifiable in some circumstances with animals. We do wrong, though, when we assume that because a creature is a non-human animal, there is no problem about sacrificing that creature's interests for the sake of human beings. To make this assumption is to deny equal consideration of interests.

Many people make a sharp distinction between humans and other animals. They say that all human beings are infinitely more valuable than any animals of any other species. But they don't give reasons for this view. When you think about it, it is not difficult to see that there is no morally important feature which *all* human beings possess, and *no* non-human animals have. We share with many other animals the capacity to suffer, and to enjoy life. And if we try to find some higher capacity, like our ability to reason, our self-awareness, or our language, we find that there are some humans – infants and the profoundly mentally damaged, for example – who do not meet this higher standard.

To a disinterested Martian, it would be amusing to see how determinedly the human species (or more specifically the Western element of that species) has tried to distance itself from the other species with which it shares the planet. Only humans, we used to say, are made in the image of God, and only humans have an immortal soul. When it became apparent that those ideas lacked any basis in reason or science, we switched to saying things like: 'Only humans can employ tools'. Then we found that chimpanzees use sticks for digging out insects, some seals will use rocks in order to break open shellfish, and various birds use thorns or small sticks to probe insects out of bark. So we said: 'Only humans *make* tools'. Then we discovered that chimpanzees do shape their sticks, by stripping off leaves and small branches until they get the right kind of implement for the task. So we switched ground and said: 'Only humans use language' – just before several studies proved that chimpanzees and gorillas could learn hundreds of signs in the sign language used by the deaf, and could communicate in quite complex ways. Of course, we then upped the requirements for what it was to use language ... and so the story goes on.

But all of these attempts at drawing lines are really quite irrelevant to the question of justifying the things we do to animals. After all, even if no animals could use tools, or communicate by means of signs or words, we could not use these abilities to draw a line between *all* humans and the non-human animals. For as we have just noticed, there are many humans, too, who cannot use tools and have no language – all humans under three months of age, for a start. And even if they are excluded on the grounds that they have the *potential* to learn to use tools and to speak, there are humans born with brain damage so severe that they will never be able to use a tool or learn any form of language.

If it would be absurd to give animals the right to vote, it would be no less absurd to give that right to infants or to severely retarded human beings. Yet we still give equal

consideration to their interests. We don't raise them for food, or test new cosmetics in their eyes. Nor should we. But we do these things to non-human animals who show greater abilities in using tools, or learning language, or doing any of the other things which use those capacities of reason that we like to believe distinguish humans from animals.

Once we understand this, it is easy to see the belief that all humans are somehow infinitely more valuable than any animal for what it is: a prejudice. Such prejudices are not unusual. Racists have a similar prejudice in favour of their own race, and sexists have the same type of prejudice in favour of their own sex. Animal liberationists use the term 'speciesism' to refer to the prejudice many humans have in favour of their own species.

Speciesism is logically parallel to racism and sexism. Speciesists, racists and sexists all say: the boundary of my own group is also the boundary of my concern. Never mind what you are like, if you are a member of my group, you are superior to all those who are not members of my group. The speciesist favours a larger group than the racist, and so has a larger circle of concern; but all of these prejudices are equally wrong. They all use an arbitrary and morally irrelevant fact – membership of a race, sex or species – as if it were morally crucial.

The only acceptable limit to our moral concern is the point at which there is no awareness of pain or pleasure, and no preferences of any kind. That is why pigs have rights, but lettuces don't. Pigs can feel pain and pleasure. Lettuces can't.

There is one final objection which should be mentioned. Since many animals kill other animals, why shouldn't we kill them as well? After all, aren't we animals too?

We are animals, of course. But animal liberationists have never denied that normal adult human beings are different from other animals in some respects. One important difference is that we have the capacity to think about what we are doing, and to make choices. That is why it makes sense to blame a human being for choosing to kill, but it would make no sense to blame a lion. The lion cannot reflect on the choice

between killing and not killing; we can. And presumably we do not want to give up that capacity, and simply act instinctively like the lion. If we were to do that, all morality would disappear.

In fact, even if the lion could reflect, it would be worse for us to kill for food than for the lion to do so. As Plutarch pointed out nearly two thousand years ago, what for the carnivorous lion is the only possible means of survival is, for the omnivorous human, mere luxury.

The ethic of animal liberation is far-reaching, but it has a sound rational basis. It has now been supported by many philosophers and thinkers, especially in Britain, North America and Australia. It has led to the rise of the modern animal liberation movement which within the space of ten years has grown to become an international force for change in the way we treat animals.

CHAPTER THREE

What we do to animals

The last chapter looked at speciesism as an *attitude*. In this chapter we look at speciesism *in practice*. It is not a pretty story, but it is essential to tell it, because it is what animal liberation is all about.

● Wildlife

In 1598 Admiral van Neck, a Dutch explorer, landed on the island of Mauritius. He reported seeing abundant flocks of a large flightless bird, bigger than a swan and unlike any bird he had seen before. The bird was the dodo. Van Neck and his crew tried eating it, but didn't much like the taste. Soon other Dutch ships followed, and brought colonists. Some of the newcomers found the taste of the dodo more appealing. Others apparently considered it sport to kill the birds with wooden clubs, despite the fact that since the bird had had no enemies it was not afraid of predators and did not attempt to run away. In any case, it could neither fly nor run quickly. The last report of a sighting of a living dodo was in 1681. It had taken Europeans only 83 years to destroy them all.

The tragic story of the dodo has been repeated all over the world. The Great Auk, a kind of Northern Hemisphere penguin, was slaughtered by the million for its feathers, to make pillows and eiderdowns. Steller's sea cow, a marine mammal which grew up to 10 metres long, was discovered on the Aleutian Islands, off Alaska, in 1741. Steller, the naturalist who discovered them, wrote that they showed 'signs of a wonderful intelligence, indeed an uncommon love

53

for one another, which extended so far that when one of them was hooked, all the others were intent upon saving it'. But their intelligence and concern for each other could not help the slow-moving animals, who were exterminated even more quickly than the dodo. By 1768 there were no more.

In the early 1800s the American passenger pigeon existed in such large numbers that the naturalist John Audubon described immense flocks blackening the sky for days at a time during their annual migration. Hunting and the destruction of habitat soon changed that. The last passenger pigeon died in the Cincinnati Zoo in 1914.

Extinction is an irreversible result of speciesism. As these examples show, the human attitude to wildlife has generally been that it is there for us to kill. It is by good luck, rather than any concern for animals, that we have avoided pushing many other species over the brink. The bison, for instance, once roamed the American plains in herds so large that they took several days to ride past. When 'Buffalo Bill' and his ilk finally

were forced to stop the slaughter, there were 22 left. The blue whale, the largest creature ever to live on this planet, was hunted until there were so few that it was no longer worth the trouble of finding them; then they were protected. We still do not know if enough have survived for the population to recover.

Today there is more concern about extinction: there are international conventions which are supposed to stop trade in furs, skins or other products from animals like the snow leopard, the tiger, the rhinoceros, and many others. But illegal poaching and trading in these products continues; and the laws do nothing to stop the destruction of the forests and jungles in which so many of the animals live. As you read this, rain forest is being cleared at a rate which has been estimated to be between one and two acres every second – think how much more will have gone in the time it has taken you to read this brief book! Nearly two hundred species of bird, mammal, reptile and amphibian have become extinct since Western civilisation began spreading over the globe in the sixteenth century; half of these extinctions have taken place in the past 100 years. *The Endangered Species Handbook* lists 354 species of mammals now in danger of extinction, as well as 209 species of birds, 77 reptiles and 17 amphibian species.

● The other wildlife issue

In any case, it is wrong to worry about the slaughter of wild animals only if the animals are in danger of extinction. People sometimes talk as if it is perfectly all right to hit baby seals over the head to make sealskin slippers, just as long as there are still going to be enough seals left to ensure that the species continues. But the seals that are killed lose their lives and future pleasures just as surely if there are a million remaining seals or if there are a dozen; and the mothers who watch their infants die will suffer just as much too.

Think about whaling.

Each year the International Whaling Commission meets to assess how many of each species of whale there are. It then allocates killing quotas to the whaling nations. The debate is always over whether the whale 'stocks' are threatened, and how many whales can be 'harvested' without reducing the 'maximum sustainable yield' for future years.

Whales might as well be floating, self-renewing reservoirs of blubber and oil, to be exploited for our maximum convenience. In discussing whale numbers, we ignore the fact that whales are living their own lives, and very likely enjoying them; we ignore the fact that they are mammals, and social animals, so that the death of one may cause a sense of loss in others; and we ignore the sheer agony that an exploding harpoon must cause in such a huge creature when, as often happens, the harpoon misses the heart and the whale takes up to twenty minutes to die.

Commercial whaling is a classic example of speciesism. We do not *need* to kill whales. There are alternatives for all whale products. In Japan, where whale flesh is eaten, it amounts to

less than 1% of the protein of the Japanese diet, and much of this is sold in expensive restaurants to people who are already eating more protein than their bodies can use. To kill whales when we do not have to do so is to place our convenience and pleasure above their lives and sufferings.

It would be wrong to think, however, that these speciesist attitudes are limited to the whaling nations like Japan and the Soviet Union. All over the world, wild animals are treated as a 'resource' to be 'harvested'. The annual bloody slaughter of baby seals on the Canadian ice seems to be over, at least for the moment, because of pressure from environmental and animal activists; but other wildlife kills which have not been so well publicised are often even larger, and no less cruel.

The kangaroo is Australia's national emblem, but that does not stop the commercial shooters. With government approval, more than two million are killed each year, to be made into car seat covers, rugs, gloves and pet food. In the United States, according to Don Atyeo's book *Blood and Guts*, 2,600,000 deer are shot by hunters each year, as well as 24,000 bears, 55,000 caribou, 67,000 moose, 102,000 elk, and an incredible 115 million birds. When we take into account other animals trapped, poisoned and killed as 'nuisances' or 'just for fun', Atyeo estimates that 250 million wild animals are deliberately killed by people in the United States during a single year – which means that eight animals are dying *every* second.

Although death by shooting is by no means always instantaneous, animals who are shot are more fortunate than those who are trapped. The steel-jawed leghold trap is widely used in North America for trapping beavers, otters, raccoons, squirrels and coyotes. In Australia, dingoes, feral dogs, and rabbits are the main targets. The trap works in this way:

when the animal, lured by a bait, places its foot on the pad of the trap, two large steel jaws with sharp serrated edges spring up and close with great force on the animal's leg. The force of the trap may be enough to break the leg; if not, the terrified animal will invariably struggle desperately, making the wound worse. Some animals try to chew their leg off in order to escape. Short of this, there is no way out. Most trapped animals are nocturnal, and as daylight comes they will be terrified at being unable to get out of the open. In hot climates their thirst becomes desperate, and may kill them. Only death, or the return of the trapper – which means the same

thing – can end their suffering. But even this release can be a long time coming: in remote regions trappers only check their traps once a week.

Anyone who buys a fur from a trapped animal is contributing to the continued use of this barbarous device. (Don't be mollified, though, by the assurance that a fur came from a 'farmed' or 'ranched' animal – farmed fur animals die more quickly, but they have a far worse life, as we show later in this chapter).

Hunters say that animals need to be 'controlled' and that many of them will die painful deaths anyway even if they are not hunted. Certainly many animals die painful deaths without any human intervention. But that is no reason for us to add to the pain. And in any case, there are no other animals which hold their prey in a wounding trap for a week. Nor has any other kind of animal been responsible for the extinction of so many species in what is, in evolutionary terms, the mere blink of an eye.

● Experimenting on animals

The experimenter cuts into the swollen abdomen of the pregnant baboon. He removes the 20-week old fetus and slits the infant's throat to insert a catheter. He then cuts open the jugular vein in order to insert another catheter. He twirls a drill bit through the infant's forehead to insert yet another catheter and drills a hole in the skull to implant electrodes into the infant's brain. In all, a total of 10 monitoring devices are placed into the infant before she is placed back into her mother's womb. The mother is then confined in a 'restraining chair' where she will spend the rest of her pregnancy.

Over the next few weeks, experimenters inject various drugs, either directly into the fetus or into the mother, in order to monitor the effect the drugs have on the infant. But all does not go according to plans. One evening, after the experimenters leave, the mother goes into labour and the baby strangles to death. Experimenters report that:

The baboons like to give birth when no one is around. Because of the (restraining) chair, and the catheters and electrodes, they can't properly tend to the infants ... and they die.

This experiment has been going on since 1968 at Columbia University's Medical School in New York. The experimenters report that as many as half of the pregnancies end with the death of the infant.

In 1986, due to public outcry, this experiment and over a hundred others were suspended by the federal government, which was supporting them. Columbia Medical School, part of one of the most prestigious universities in the US, was found to be in flagrant violation of the minimal guidelines set by the National Institutes of Health. These guidelines say nothing about what may or may not be done to an animal during the course of an experiment, for they are concerned primarily with 'good house-keeping practices' such as cleanliness, cage sizes and ventilation. As a result of the suspension, the thousands of animals used at Columbia won a temporary reprieve. Millions of others who suffer and die in laboratories are not so lucky.

Although no exact figures are available (a result, perhaps, of the secrecy under which animal experimentation is performed) it has been estimated that as many as 70 million animals are killed in US laboratories every year. That is over 100 animals in the time it takes to read this paragraph. In Britain, where the government publishes official figures, the number is 3.3 million. Even this much smaller number is equivalent to nearly 10,000 animals a day, or more than 6 animals every minute.

These animals, including dogs, cats, monkeys, mice, rats, pigs, and others, often suffer extreme pain, terror and loneliness in experiments which are sanctioned by governments, and frequently subsidised by every taxpayer, through government grants.

66

In most so-called civilized nations, under the guise of 'scientific inquiry', animals are suffocated, starved, shocked, blinded, burned, beaten, frozen, decapitated, electrocuted and killed. In many countries, including the United States, noxious procedures can legally be performed on any animals, in any laboratory, for any reason – without the use of pain-killers.

'But surely', you may say, 'animal experiments are performed only where necessary to save human lives!' But the sad truth is, despite what experimenters would like us to believe, that most, if not all animal experiments have nothing to do with saving lives. Consider the following experiments, carried out recently at highly respected research institutions:

● At Harvard University, researchers cut away the edges of the eyelids (plus lashes) of 47 infant monkeys. The remaining lids were then sewn together. In some cases this was done on one eye, in some cases on both. In addition:

> two monkeys with one eye closed were reared in the dark for 10 and 12 months;
> two monkeys had a suspension of polystyrene beads injected into one cornea at birth to render them opaque;
> in seven monkeys the lid closure was left incomplete, and atropine was installed daily;
> seven monkeys had optic nerves severed.

After about a year the monkeys had their eyes opened and examined. The researchers found that these procedures made the monkeys short-sighted to varying degrees, but they could not explain the variation. They noted that different species of monkeys seemed to have different mechanisms for the development of short-sightedness, and added: 'Better, more controlled ways of interfering with form vision must be devised ... ' They referred to 23 papers reporting at least 16 separate studies, on different species, that have looked at the same or similar effects. (E. Raviola and T. Wiesel, 'An Animal Model of Myopia', *New England Journal of Medicine* 312 (1985), 1609-15.)

- At the Massachusetts Institute of Technology, monkeys were placed in special holding devices in order to study their visual mechanisms. Their heads were held rigidly by bolts implanted in their skulls. The animals then had parts of their eyeballs liquefied, either by the injection of drugs or with the use of a small wire whisk inserted into the eyeball and 'twirled around much like a miniature egg beater'. The experimenters admitted that their techniques had limitations which meant that for part of the work 'quantitative data across animals could not be collected meaningfully'. Other data could not support generalisation, so experimenters suggested that 'a larger sample will be necessary'. (P. Schiller, 'The Connection of the Retinal On and Off Pathways of the Geniculate Nucleus of the Monkey', *Vision Research* 24 (1984), 923-932.)

- In a four-year study at Northwestern University one group of rats was trained by being rewarded when they performed a required task, while another group was constantly frustrated by electric shocks, regardless of whether or not they behaved 'properly'. Rats from the first 'optimistic group' and rats from the second 'depressed group' were then placed in a vat of water from which they could not escape. The experimenters found that after struggling for a short period of time, the 'depressed' rats 'give up' and sink to the bottom. The 'optimistic' rats tend

to struggle until they become exhausted and drown. This was said to show that depressed rats tend to be more realistic than optimistic rats. (*The Washington Post,* March 29, 1981.)

● Researchers from the University of Colorado and New Mexico State University were aware of an experiment which found that young chimpanzees kept in isolation 'reacted with high levels of "protest" alternating with "despair" throughout the separation period'. They thought it would be interesting to see if this happened with infant chimpanzees. so they used seven infant chimpanzees who had been removed from their mothers at birth and raised in a group nursery environment. After 7-10 months, some of the infants were placed in isolation chambers. The isolated infants screamed, rocked, and threw themselves at the walls of the chamber. From this the experimenters learned that 'peer separation (and isolation) in infant

IT'S NOT THE CAT WHO NEEDS HIS HEAD EXAMINED

chimpanzees may be accompanied by marked behavioural changes'. They also said that 'A more definitive study ... would appear warranted' (D. Snyder, C. Graham, J. Brown and M. Reite, 'Peer Separation in Infant Chimpanzees, a Pilot Study', *Primates* 25 (1) (January 1984), 78-88.)

- At the University of Wisconsin experimenters gave electric shocks to 160 rats. Some were allowed to escape the shock, others were not. The experimenters declared that 'our conclusions raise some questions about the validity of the conclusions of the hundreds of experiments conducted over the past 15 years or so that have compared the effects of controllable versus uncontrollable shock on a variety of dependent variables' (S. Mineka, M. Cok and S. Miller, 'Fear Conditioned with Escapable and Inescapable Shock: Effects of a Feedback Stimulus', *Journal of Experimental Psychology: Animal Behavior* 10(3) (1984), 307-323.)

- At the University of Wisconsin, ducks had their wings intentionally broken to determine whether crippled ducks could survive in the wild. All but one bird died from starvation, exposure, predation, or a combination of factors. (*Philadelphia Inquirer,* December 30, 1982.)

- At the University of Texas, kittens were injected with LSD to study their behaviour. The kittens became uncoordinated, vomited, salivated, and displayed frequent body spasms. The experimenters reported that LSD 'produced a constellation of behavioural signs that has been previously described in detail' (M. Trulson and G. Howell, 'Ontogeny of the Behavioural Effects of LSD in Cats', *Developmental Psychobiology* 17 (1984), 329-346.)

- In England, the Huntingdon Research Institute, together with the giant corporation ICI, carried out experiments in which 40 monkeys were poisoned with the week-killer paraquat. They became very ill, vomited, had difficulty in breathing and suffered from hypothermia. They died slowly, over several days. It was already known that paraquat poisoning in humans results in a slow and agonising death. (D.A. Purser and M.S. Rose, 'The Toxicity and Renal Handling of Paraquat in Cynomolgous monkeys', *Toxicology* 15 (1)(1979), 31-41.)

● In Newcastle, England, castrated mini-pigs (a new type of pig specially bred for laboratory use, in part because experiments on pigs are considered less likely to upset the public than experiments on dogs) were subjected to up to eighty-one periods of compression and decompression. All the pigs suffered attacks of decompression sickness, from which several died. (*British Journal of Experimental Pathology* 61 (1980), 39; cited by Richard Ryder, 'Speciesism in the Laboratory' in P.Singer (ed.) *In Defence of Animals*, p. 81.)

● In Hertfordshire, England, electric shocks were repeatedly administered to the tooth pulp of beagle dogs which were injected with various substances including, in some cases, analgesics. (*British Journal of Pharmacology* 70 (1980); cited by Richard Ryder, as above.)

● At Dalhousie University in Canada, kittens were removed from their mothers at birth and placed in complete darkness for up to two years. These and other cats then had one eye sewn up. The animals were then killed and their brains dissected. The conclusion: depriving cats of vision in one eye was 'more effective' when the cats had been reared in darkness. (M. Cynader, 'Prolapsed sensitivity to monocular deprivation in dark-reared cats: effects of age and visual exposure', *Brain Research* 284 (June 1983), 155-64.)

● At the University of Melbourne Veterinary Clinical Centre, in Australia, nine dogs were poisoned with lead. They developed the usual well-known symptoms of lead poisoning, including diarrhoea, vomiting, lethargy, and fits which lasted nearly an hour. One dog became dehydrated and died; others died during their fits. The aim of the experiment was said to be 'to study the brain injury which follows exposure to lead compounds and to refine criteria for the diagnosis of lead poisoning in dogs' (Department of Agriculture, Government of Victoria,

Investigation into the Administration of Lead Salts to Dogs
(February 1983).

● At the Cumberland College of Health Sciences, in Sydney, Australia, 42 dogs repeatedly had a starting pistol fired close to their heads. This procedure 'clearly upset all subjects'. The dogs 'urinated, screamed and struggled'. Some were subjected to 60 or 70 such 'trials'. The conclusion: 'Generalizations from animal analogues need to the treated cautiously, but there does seem to be some reason to take into account the disinhibition hypothesis when planning treatment of phobias' (M. Pryke, 'The Disinhibitory Effect of Arousal on Fear Responses', *Australian Journal of Psychology* 32 (2)(1980), 111-115.)

• 'Conditioned ethical blindness'

How can otherwise decent citizens do these things? How can they become so insensitive to what they are doing? Don Barnes, who spent sixteen years as a biomedical scientist experimenting on animals, and now heads the Washington, DC office of the National Anti-Vivisection Society, calls the state in which he used to do his work 'conditioned ethical blindness'.

From his early years growing up on the farm, and continuing into his time as a Ph.D student, Barnes accepted the idea that non-human animals exist to serve human purposes. As a student of psychology, he was also taught a whole new vocabulary which served to distance the experimenter from the animal. The monkeys on which he worked became 'research subjects'; the electric shocks he gave them were called 'negative reinforcement' and their vain efforts to escape were classified as 'avoidance behaviour'. As Barnes says: 'During my sixteen years in the laboratory the morality and ethics of using laboratory animals were never broached in either formal or informal meetings prior to my raising the issues during the waning days of my tenure as a vivisector'.

Don Barnes is not the only one to have escaped his conditioning. In 1977 the magazine *Monitor*, published by the American Psychological Association, reported that experiments on aggression carried out by Roger Ulrich had been singled out before a Congressional subcommittee as an example of inhuman research. In a response that must have surprised the Editor of *Monitor*, Ulrich wrote back to say that he was 'heartened' by the criticism of his research; and he added:

> **Initially my research was prompted by the desire to understand and help solve the problem of human aggression, but I later discovered that the results of my work did not seem to justify its continuance. Instead I began to wonder if perhaps financial rewards, professional prestige, the opportunity to travel, etc.**

were the maintaining factors, and if we of the scientific community (supported by our bureaucratic and legislative system) were actually a part of the problem ...

When I finished my dissertation on pain-produced aggression, my Mennonite mother asked me what it was about. When I told her she replied, 'Well, we knew that. Dad always warned us to stay away from animals in pain because they are more likely to attack'. Today I look back with love and respect on all my animal friends from rats to monkeys who submitted to years of torture so that like my mother I can say, 'Well, we know that ...'

● Proving the obvious

When presented with examples of mindless animal experiments, scientists usually claim that we, as lay-people, do not understand the importance of their work. But the fact is that, like Ulrich's, many animal experiments are performed merely to prove the obvious. Nowhere is this more true than in experimental psychology.

Among the best-known psychology experiments are those of H.F. Harlow, who in the late 1950s began a series of maternal deprivation experiments at the University of Wisconsin Primate Research Centre. The first experiments involved the separation of a baby monkey from her mother in order to study 'the nature of love'. Harlow devised fake 'monkey mothers', one made of cloth and one made of wire. Not surprisingly, all infants showed a preference for the more comfortable, cloth-covered 'mother'. Harlow concluded that comfort has a role in the formation of bonds between infants and their mothers.

Harlow and his colleagues then proceeded to modify the surrogate mothers in order to produce bizarre behaviour in infant monkeys:

> ... **four surrogate monster mothers were created. One**
> **was a shaking mother which rocked so violently that the**
> **teeth and bones of the infant chattered in unison. The**
> **second was an air-blast mother which blew compressed**
> **air against the infant's face and body with such violence**
> **that the infant looked as if it would be denuded. The**
> **third had an embedded steel frame which, on schedule**
> **or demand, would fling forward and knock the infant**
> **monkey off the mother's body. The fourth monster**
> **mother, on schedule or demand, ejected brass spikes**
> **from her ventral surface, an abominable form of**
> **maternal tenderness** ...
>
> (H. Harlow, *Learning to Love*, New York, Aronson, 1974,
> p.38.)

Terrifying as the monster monkeys were, the unfortunate infants continued to return to them, no doubt because they had no other source of comfort.

Over the next two decades, Harlow moved away from studying 'affection' in favour of creating a 'primate model of depression'. He created such horrors as the 'well of despair', 'the tunnel of terror', and living 'monster' mothers who had themselves been brought up in isolation, and had developed such antisocial behaviour that they had to be forcibly tied down in 'rape racks' in order to be mated. These experiments, and similar ones still being carried out today by Harlow's former students, epitomise the deliberate abuse of animals which occurs in some laboratories.

Experimental psychology raises, in an especially acute form, a central contradiction of much animal experimentation. For if the monkeys Harlow used do not crave affection like human infants, and if they do not experience loneliness, terror and despair like human infants, what is the point of the experiments? But if the monkeys do crave affection, and do feel loneliness, terror and despair in the way that humans do, how can the experiments possibly be justified?

HARRY HARLOW INTRODUCES A BABY RHESUS MONKEY TO ITS MONSTER MOTHER...

● Again and again and again …

So ingrained is the pattern of animal experimentation that
thousands of animals suffer and die in experiments which are
merely minor variations on work that has been done many
times before. According to a study done by the New York
group, United Action for Animals, in the past 60 years
experiments in which animals were forced to consume alcohol
have been performed at least 850 times, asphyxiation
experiments 875 times, and burn experiments 650 times.
Animals have been terrorised in fear experiments 700 times,

and blinded 600 times. Over 775 experiments studied aggression, 1400 sexual behaviour in primates, 550 examined taste aversion, and no fewer than 38,000 have tested the carcinogenicity of radiation. These figures refer to separate experiments; each experiment may have used tens, and sometimes hundreds, of animals.

This kind of repetition is a common occurrence, accepted by scientists. Lewis Thomas, the author of *Lives of a Cell* and once head of the Sloan-Kettering Cancer Research Institute, noted while reflecting on an experiment he had performed on rabbits:

> **Then, of course, I made the usual illuminating discovery, the commonest epiphany in research: someone else had done my experiments** (*The Youngest Science*, **p.153.**)

● Deliberate poisoning

Over 20 million animals die slow, agonising deaths every year in tests performed purely for profit. These animals die in experiments conducted before any product is put on the market. Substances such as motor oil, talcum powder, hair spray, toothpaste, nail polish remover, antifreeze, window cleaner and new shades of eyeshadow are placed in animals' eyes, noses and rectums, or are fed to animals in toxicity tests, the two most common of which are the Draize eye irritancy test and the Acute oral toxicity test.

The Draize eye irritancy tests are left over from the 1940s, when J.H. Draize, working for the US Food and Drug Administration, developed a scale for assessing how irritating a substance is when placed in a rabbit's eye. In general, rabbits are placed in restraining stocks so that they cannot scratch at their eyes. A substance (such as liquid bleach, or a shampoo or mascara) is then placed in one of the rabbit's eyes by pulling out the lower lid and placing the substance into the small 'cup' thus formed. The eye is then held closed and, depending on how the substance affects the eye, the rabbit may scream in pain and struggle desperately, but in vain, to free herself.

The animal is observed daily for eye swelling, ulceration, infection, and bleeding. The studies can last up to three weeks. Some substances cause such serious damage that the rabbit's eye loses all distinguishing characteristics - her iris, pupil, and cornea begin to resemble one massive infection. Experimenters are not obliged to use an anaesthetic, but sometimes they will use a minute amount of topical anaesthesia when introducing the substance, provided it does not interfere with the test. Of course, this does nothing to alleviate the excruciating pain that can result after two weeks of having oven cleaner in the eye. At the end of the study the rabbits are killed and discarded.

In oral toxicity tests, which have been going on since the 1920s, animals are forced to ingest substances, including such non-edible products as lipstick or paper. Beagles and rats are widely used for this test. Often they will not eat the substance if it is placed in their food, so experimenters either force-feed the animals by mouth or insert a tube down their throats. Standard tests are carried out for 14 days but some may last for up to six months if the animals don't die sooner. During that time, animals often display classic symptoms of poisoning: vomiting, diarrhoea, paralysis, convulsions, and internal bleeding.

One common way of assessing the toxicity of any test substance is to find the 'LD50' value. LD50 stands for Lethal Dose 50%, the amount of the substance that will kill half of

the animals in a study. To find that dose level, sample groups of animals are poisoned. Normally, before the point at which half of them die is reached, they are all very ill and in obvious distress. In the late 1970s, animal rights activists began to protest against the LD50 test. After years of struggle they forced commercial manufacturers to re-examine its use. Today companies claim that they are not using the LD50 and that they have reduced the number of animals they poison. In fact, they still use the same methods in 'range finding' tests, many of which kill 50%, 75% and even 100% of the animals used.

Animals are not only forced to ingest substances or have substances placed in their eyes in toxicity testing. Other tests include:

- inhalation studies, in which animals are placed in vapour chambers. Often the animals die, not from inhaling the substance but by absorbing the substance through their skin.
- dermal toxicity studies, in which animals, usually rabbits, have their fur removed so that various substances can be placed on their skin. The animals are restrained so that they do not scratch their irritated bodies. In many cases, the skin begins to blister and peel and the test is continued until half the animals die.
- immersion studies, in which animals are placed in vats of diluted substances for various periods of time over the course of the study. Many animals drown before the study is over.
- injection studies, in which substances are injected under the skin, into muscles, or into different organs to determine their effect.

The results of these crude, painful toxicity tests are in any case unreliable. Scientists have criticized the use of such tests because the results can be affected by the age, sex and species of the animals, their diets, the temperature, the stress of the experiments, and even the stress produced by the barren laboratory environment itself. But toxicity studies are not the

only studies susceptible to these criticisms. Extrapolation from one species to another is a problem for all animal experiments and placing reliance on animal tests often leads to a drug or other product harming human beings.

● Results from one species can't be applied to another species.

Remember the thalidomide tragedy? Thalidomide was a non-essential sleeping pill that was released on the market after three years of extensive testing on dogs, cats, mice, rats, rabbits, hamsters and monkeys, but which led to the birth of thousands of deformed children. Unfortunately humans proved to be more susceptible to the drug than other animals. The story is similar for DES, Oraflex, Zomax, Eraldin, and a host of other drugs that were tested on animals and released on the market, causing illness, cancer, and even death in the humans who took them or the children they were carrying.

Different species respond differently. Insulin produces deformities in rabbits. Almonds kill foxes. Cats are allergic to aspirin. Parsley is poisonous to parrots. Morphine, which is calming to man, causes mice to go into frenzies. Penicillin is lethal to guinea pigs. On the other hand, sheep can eat enormous quantities of arsenic without becoming ill and porcupines can eat more opium than it takes to kill a human. As well as exposing people to harm, testing on animals may lead us to miss out on valuable products that are dangerous for animals but not for us.

Some animal experimenters are beginning to recognise that animals are similar to us in morally relevant ways, and have long since known that using results from animal experiments is risky. Nonetheless, they claim that they must perform the experiments but consider them a 'necessary evil'. As we have seen, most animal experiments have nothing to do with promoting human health. But if experimenters believe their experiments would produce benefits, then from a moral point of view they should be willing to perform the experiments on mentally retarded humans with the same

It has been estimated that between 100 million and 200 million animals die in laboratories around the world each year.

The best statistics have been kept by the Home Office in Britain, where the 1986 figures reveal that 3,280,135 experiments on living animals were licensed in the previous year. Of these, most involved the testing or development of veterinary, medical or dental drugs and other products, but 50,811 were for the testing of pesticides, 27,823 for the testing of herbicides, 58,856 for the testing of substances for industry, 9,807 for testing household substances, 16,625 for the testing of cosmetics and toiletries, 14,752 for the testing of food additives, and 2103 for testing tobacco and its substitutes. The experiments were performed mainly on rodents (1,724,616 mice, 884,343 rats, 135,907 guinea pigs, 151,530 rabbits) but included 5869 on primates (monkeys or apes), 12,721 on dogs, 164,108 on birds and 6,428 on cats.

Experiments involving the deliberate induction of psychological stress numbered 20,640; 1,839 involved burning or scalding; 111,626 involved exposure to ionizing radiation; 33,039 involved the use of aversive stimuli such as electric shock; 12,983 involved the application of substances to the eye; and 82,045 involved interference with the brain or other parts of the central nervous system. 76.3% of all experiments were carried out without anaesthetic.

('Statistics of Experiments on Living Animals, Great Britain, 1985' (Cmnd 9839).)

capacities as the animals. (Scientifically, the experiment would have more meaning for humans if performed on a member of our own species). Scientists are rightly unwilling to experiment on these human beings; but if they still maintain that the experiments must be done on animals, then they reveal an arbitrary prejudice against beings not of our species, a prejudice not unlike the one which allowed white people to enslave – and, incidentally, to experiment on – black people.

● Alternatives do exist

'But medical progress would come to a standstill!', the defenders of animal experimentation will say. In fact, we would all benefit if instead of trying to make healthy animals sick, we used the money on preventing illness by encouraging a healthy lifestyle. Consider cancer. Every year, literally billions of dollars are spent trying to create an animal 'model' of cancer. Thousands of animals, from rats to dogs to monkeys, have been killed in a hopeless effort to find the ever-elusive cure for cancer.

What have we got for the billions of dollars and countless animal suffering? Last year more people died from cancer than the year before. We already know that 65% of all cancers are environmentally caused and that the chance of getting cancer would be greatly diminished by changes in lifestyle. If animal experimentation was not such an old habit and money was redirected, educating the public about early detection and simple prevention, more people would live healthier lives.

Ironically, the failure of the 'animal model' method of eliminating cancer was predicted some fifteen years (and how many millions of pounds?) ago in an article in the leading British medical journal, *The Lancet*, for April 15, 1972:

> **Most of the (anti-cancer) agents now in use were first tested in tumour-bearing animals, particularly rodents with transplanted tumours. Clearly, however, this method has its limitations. As in human beings, there is**

great variability in the response of different tumour lines to different agents. Since no animal tumour is closely related to a cancer in a human being, an agent which is active in the laboratory may well prove to be useless clinically.

There are other, often more efficient and reliable, methods available to animal experimenters. Computer and mathematical modelling, and the use of cell and tissue cultures, are some of the methods which can be pursued.

The problem is that animal experimentation is big business. Huge corporations, such as Charles Rivers Breeding Laboratories, which supplies not only animals, but cages, food, and experimentation tools, stand to lose billions of dollars if animal experimentation comes to an end. Individual

93

experimenters, having built their careers on experimenting, also have great incentives to continue experimenting on animals. Often they need outside grants if they want to keep their jobs. Since animal experimentation is all they know and since funding agencies tend to ignore innovative, productive, non-animal research proposals, in favour of the status quo, the experimenters really don't have much of an option.

But the fundamental reason why animal experimentation continues is because the companies who profit from it, the individuals who must experiment or lose their jobs, and the funding agencies who have made it a habit, are all acting on their arbitrary prejudice against feeling, thinking animals. They are speciesists, and until they throw away their indefensible prejudice and begin to address the fundamental moral issue, the needless suffering will continue.

● Food animals

When do you most often have contact with non-human animals? Probably at meal times, when the animals are served up dead on a plate. But how often do we think that what appears on our plate was once a living, breathing, feeling animal? And how much do we know about how that animal lived and died?

'As often as Herman had witnessed the slaughter of animals and fish, he always had the same thought: in their behaviour towards creatures, all men were Nazis. The smugness with which man could do with other species as he pleased exemplified the most extreme racist theories, the principle that might is right.'

(from 'Enemies, A Love Story', by the Nobel Prize-winning author, Isaac Bashevis Singer.)

'Don't tell me, it will spoil my dinner!' is the most common reaction to any attempt to describe the conditions of food animals. But those who don't want to know about anything disturbing resemble those Germans who helped ship Jews to concentration camps and didn't want to know about what happened to them there. When we buy and eat meat, or other animal products, we are giving tacit approval and financial support to the way in which animals are treated by modern technology. We ought to be prepared to learn what those methods are like.

● Animal factories

For a start, forget about those story-book images of hens scratching around the yard, and pigs wallowing in the mud. The last twenty years has seen 'factory farming' spread throughout the industrialised world. Factory farming, also known as intensive farming, is a system of keeping animals

96

indoors, in large sheds, where every aspect of their existence can be regulated to produce the maximum output at the minimum cost. Pigs, chickens, turkeys, egg-laying hens and veal calves are now kept in this way.

Factory farming is big business. Small family farms have been pushed out by 'agribusiness' - huge corporations for which raising animals is just a profitable form of investment. It is not only the large sheds which make the term 'factory' so apt. The animals themselves are forced into the role of a machine in a factory: you put the cheap raw materials (grain, with antibiotics, growth promotants and other artificial additives) into the machine, and the machine turns them into finished products (pork, eggs, poultry etc.) which can be sold at a profit. Anything that *can* be done to make the machine work more efficiently *will* be done.

Twenty years ago Ruth Harrison described the new production methods in her ground-breaking book *Animal Machines*. The theme of the book was summed up in one key sentence: 'Cruelty is only acknowledged where profitability ceases'. That sentence is as true today as it was when Ruth Harrison wrote it.

Here are some of the conditions under which animals now live:

● **Hens**

The hens which lay our eggs live in wire cages. A cage which houses four or even five hens is typically 12 by 18 inches (30 by 45 cm), and barely high enough for the hens to stand up in. Measure it out and you'll see that it is no larger than a single page of a daily newspaper. Sometimes four hens are kept in a cage as small as 12 by 12 inches, which is the size of the cover of a record album.

Suppose we take the larger of these cages, and assume that it holds four, not five, hens. Then each of these large birds has 54 square inches (337.5 sq cm). For comparison, a *single* page of this book is 8 by 6 inches, which means that it has an area of

'The modern layer is, after all, only a very efficient converting machine, changing the raw material – feeding stuffs – into the finished product – the egg – less, of course, maintenance requirements.'

('Farmer and Stockbreeder', a leading British farming magazine, expressing the basic attitude that resulted in the animal factory boom, January 30, 1962.)

48 square inches (294 sq cm), and conditions can be a lot worse. When four hens are forced to live in a 12 by 12 inch cage, each bird has only 36 square inches (225 sq cm) of space.

The hens are imprisoned in these cages from the time they are ready to start laying until their rate of laying eggs drops off and the factory manager decides that it is time to throw out the old – they may end up as chicken soup – and bring in fresh hens. This is usually after about a year, although it may be as long as eighteen months.

In these cages, the hens cannot even stretch their wings, because the wingspan of a hen is about 32 inches (82 cm). The longest straight line in a 12 by 18 inch cage, the diagonal line from one corner to the other, is less than 22 inches (54 cm).

The crowding puts the birds under great stress, which leads them to become aggressive. They peck at each other, and with their sharp beaks could easily kill the weaker birds in the cage. Do the factory managers increase the size of the cage to reduce the stress? No, because then they could not fit so many birds into each shed, and their costs would go up. Instead they cut off the sharp end of the birds' beaks. This operation used to be known as 'debeaking' but is now sometimes called 'beak trimming' by the increasingly image-conscious poultry industry. It is done with a red-hot blade. As an expert British Government committee said of this operation:

> **Between the horn and the bone (of the beak) is a thin layer of highly sensitive soft tissue, resembling the quick of the human nail. The hot knife blade used in debeaking cuts through this complex of horn, bone and sensitive tissue causing severe pain.** (*Report of the Technical Committee to Enquire into the Welfare of Animals kept under Intensive Livestock Systems,* London, HMSO, 1965.)

• Chickens

Debeaking is a routine part of every intensive egg production factory; it is also standard in the other major branch of the poultry industry, the raising of chickens for the table, or as they are known in the industry, 'broilers'. Like the hens

---

'If any person keeps or confines any bird whatsoever in any cage or other receptacle which is not sufficient in height, length or breadth to permit the bird to stretch its wings freely, he shall be guilty of an offence against the Act and be liable to a special penalty. **Provided that this sub-section shall not apply to poultry.**'

(from the Protection of Birds Act (UK).)

which lay our eggs, these birds never see the light of day. They are kept in long dim densely packed sheds which hold 10,000, 20,000 or even more birds.

Chickens are naturally social creatures. Left to themselves, they will form small flocks in which every chicken can recognise every other chicken in the flock. They establish a 'pecking order', which means that they know their place in the social hierarchy. We often think of chickens as stupid, but tests have shown that they can identify up to ninety other birds in a flock. This ability, however, is of little use when they are thrust into a shed with 10,000 other birds. Then the social system breaks down; they are constantly coming up against strange birds, and the result is extreme stress and aggression. Debeaking helps the factory manager cut the losses from this aggression, but does nothing to reduce the underlying stress.

Broilers are grown quickly and slaughtered young - nine

weeks is the longest any of them live. Yet even within that short period, 6% – or more than one in twenty – will die. Since the broiler industry in the United States produces something over 3 *billion* birds a year, this adds up to 180 *million* deaths. Such high mortality is a sign of the stress under which the chickens live, but for the broiler producers it is just part of the running costs of their system. When you are mass producing chickens, individual birds don't matter.

• Pigs

Why do people eat some animals and shun others? It cannot be anything to do with the intelligence or sensitivity of the animals, because pigs are every bit as intelligent as dogs, and just as keen on stimulation or activity.

Yet pigs are kept locked up in conditions so bad that anyone who treated a dog that way could be prosecuted. Animal factories keep all their pigs indoors. The breeding sows are the worst affected. Their role is simply to produce piglets. The piglets will be removed from their mothers as soon as possible after birth. Then the sow will be mated with a boar so that she becomes pregnant again, and the cycle can be repeated. From the factory manager's point of view the sow has no other reason for existing, and an efficient sow is one which produces a lot of piglets at little cost.

'Forget the pig is an animal. Treat him just like a machine in a factory. Schedule treatments like you would lubrication. Breeding season is like the first step in an assembly line. And marketing like the delivery of finished goods.'

(J. Byrnes, in 'Hog Farm Management', an American magazine for pig producers, September 1976.)

103

has no other reason for existing, and an efficient sow is one who produces a lot of piglets at little cost.

To keep the costs down, sows are locked into small metal stalls, measuring about 6 feet (1.8m) long by 2 feet (0.6m). This is scarcely larger than the sow herself, and does not permit her to take more than one step backwards or forwards. She cannot even turn around. This confinement prevents 'wasteful' exercise which might make the pig eat more than necessary. Sometimes instead of being in stalls, sows are tethered by a short chain around the neck. The restriction of movement is just as great. The floors are concrete, and the sows are given no straw or other bedding because that would increase costs for no economic return.

Sows must live in these barren conditions for months at a time, until they are ready to give birth. Then they are taken

out, only to be put straight into another form of confinement, the 'farrowing crate'. From there it is back to the boar, and once pregnant, back to the stall or tether. This stops only when the sow is judged to be too old to earn her keep, and then she is slaughtered.

The sow's piglets have a shorter life with a little more room to move, but always indoors, never seeing sunlight or breathing fresh air, with no stimulation except a bare concrete pen with a few other pigs.

Pigs in animal factories are frustrated and bored. Dr G. van

Putten, a scientist from the Institute of Animal Husbandry in the Netherlands, has made a life-long study of the needs of pigs and the way they behave in modern conditions. He has found that they need to be able to explore, to have stimulation of some sort, and to make themselves comfortable by bathing or lying in wet places. They also like to lie in close bodily contact with other pigs. All these needs are denied by modern systems of production.

● Veal calves

Bad as life must be for a sow in a pig factory, for a calf in a veal factory it is worse still. The typical veal factory consists of a large shed lined with bare wooden stalls. Each stall is less than 2 feet (60 cm) wide, and no more than 4½ feet (1.4m) long. It has no straw or other bedding material. In each stall stands a young calf. The calf will have been in the stall since a few days after birth, and will remain there until ready for slaughter, at about 14 weeks. The stall is too small for the calf to turn around, or walk a single step. The calf cannot even lie down comfortably.

The cramped stall prevents the calf from exercising and 'wasting' its food; but the factory manager also wants to keep the calf's flesh a pale pink colour, because so-called 'white' veal fetches a higher price. This pale colour is normal in a calf a few days old, but in natural conditions would disappear as soon as the calf begins to eat grass and obtain iron, the essential nutrient which prevents anaemia. To produce a 14 week old calf with flesh of this colour, the factory manager deliberately sets out to deprive the calves of iron and thus make them anaemic. Here is what the factory manager does:

● The water supply is checked. If it is naturally rich in iron, a filter is fitted to remove the iron.

● The calves are fed on an all-liquid skimmed milk diet, which contains very little iron. They are not fed any hay or roughage, because that would give them iron.

'The dual aims of veal production are, firstly, to produce a calf of the greatest weight in the shortest possible time and, secondly, to keep its meat as light coloured as possible to fulfil the consumer's requirement. All at a profit commensurate to the risk and investment involved.'

(from 'The Stall Street Journal', a magazine for veal producers published by Provimi, Inc., a leading American veal marketer, July 1972.)

- The calves are denied straw for bedding, because they would chew that and absorb iron from it.
- The stalls in which the calves live are made of wood, and care is taken to see that there are no iron bars, hinges or bolts anywhere the iron-hungry calves could lick them.

The calves who emerge from this system are weak and anaemic, but most of them will survive until it is time for them to be slaughtered. Then their pale flesh will be sold at a premium price to fancy restaurants.

The white veal trade rejects any concern for the well-being or health of the calf. It also wastes large quantities of food, because the high-protein skimmed milk powder on which the calves are fed could be used directly by people in need of extra protein. The only purpose of this process is to produce an expensive, luxury meat for overfed 'gourmets'.

In Roman times, the wealthy liked to dine on foetal piglets whose mother had been trampled to death while the piglets were in her womb. Roman gourmets said that the flesh of these piglets was especially delicate. The white veal trade proves that today's gourmets have yet to develop an ethical sensitivity which is superior to their predecessors.

● Factory farming spreads

No animal is safe from the rush to convert farming into agribusiness. Long after chickens and pigs had been brought indoors, dairy cows continued to graze in green meadows. Now they too are often kept tethered in a shed where they are treated like a milk-producing machine. They are fed, given antibiotics to keep them from getting infections, and twice a day their udders are pumped out through mechanical milking devices. To keep milk production high, the cows are periodically made pregnant; but when the calves are born, they are taken away from their mothers so that humans can have the milk. When, after a few pregnancies, milk production drops off permanently, the cows are sent to slaughter.

108

109

The fur industry is going the same way. Mink have been factory-reared for years; now even animals like the Arctic Fox are spending their lives in wire cages, barely able to exercise, waiting only for the day when their fur is ready to go on someone else's back.

Which animals will be next? Rabbits are already being raised in wire cages, like the battery cages in which hens live. Cattle are taken from the range and fattened in giant feedlots on grains which are unsuitable for their stomachs. They put on weight fast, but they also waste more than 90% of the food value of the grains they eat. In Australia, sheep are now being kept indoors in order to produce a superfine clean fleece which fetches extraordinarily high prices.

The trend to animal factories is a disaster for animals, for the environment and for the poor and hungry of the world, who see the food that could nourish them - much of it produced in their own countries - being converted into animal products which return a mere fraction of the food value of what the animals were fed.

● Some 'traditional' farm practices

The modern animal factories take to an extreme the attitude that animals are mere things for us to use. On the traditional family farms, animals were still individuals, and had far more freedom to move around and satisfy their natural instincts. But don't get the idea that on the more traditional farm everything is sweetness and light. Here are some quite routine procedures which are part of traditional farming methods:

● Most male cattle, sheep and pigs are *castrated*. The normal method is to pin the animal down, take a knife, slit the scrotum, and then pull on each testicle in turn until the cord breaks.

● Cattle are *branded*. Despite the alternative of modern painless marking techniques, many cattle ranchers still use the old hot iron method. The hair is clipped away first, and the red-hot iron is held against the animals' flesh for a full five seconds.

'Shut up a young boar, of a year and a half old, in a little room in harvest time, feeding him with nothing but sweet whey, and giving him every morning clean straw to lie upon, but lay it not thick; so before Christmas he will be sufficiently brawned with continued lying, and prove exceedingly fat, wholesome and sweet. And after he is brawned for your turn, thrust a knife into one of his flanks, and let him run with it till he die; others gently bait him with muzzled dogs.'

(T. Moufet, 'Health's Improvement' 1746.)

- Cattle are *de-horned*. The steer is held firmly by a device called a crush, then the horn is simply sawn off, a process which cuts through arteries and sensitive tissue as well as hard bone.
- Many farm animals are *transported* for long distances, often going without food or water for up to 36 hours. The farming industry is itself worried about the immense losses caused by bruising, injury and death in the transportation process - yet these losses continue because it seems to be cheaper to accept them than to do anything about eliminating long-distance road and rail transport.
- Finally, there is *slaughter*. The killing itself may be quick, but the animal is still liable to be terrified, fearful of the strange environment, and sensitive to the smells of death.

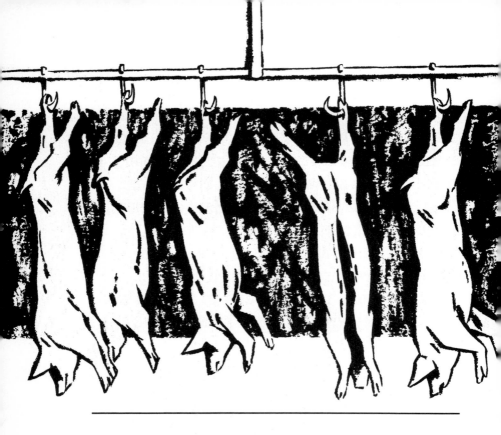

'The pen narrows like a funnel; the drivers behind urge the pigs forward, until one at a time they climb onto the moving ramp ... Now they scream, never having been on such a ramp, smelling the smells they smell ahead. I do not want to overdramatise because you have read all this before. But it was a frightening experience, seeing their fear, seeing so many of them go by; it had to remind me of things no one wants to be reminded of anymore, all mobs, all death marches, all mass murders and extinctions ... '

(Richard Rhodes, 'Watching the Animals', 'Harpers', March 1970.)

CHAPTER FOUR

What are we going to do about it?

Sometimes we would like to stop something that is wrong, but there is little we can do about it because the wrong is being done so far away from us. It is hard to do more than make token gestures towards stopping the evils of apartheid, say, or the denial of human rights in the Soviet Union. We can refuse to participate in sporting or other contacts with these countries, but we cannot directly make a difference towards improving the lives of oppressed people in these countries, because we are not ourselves involved in the oppression.

Animal liberation isn't like that. Animals are being denied proper consideration, and you *are* involved in it. Unless you are one of the few already committed to the idea of animal liberation, and following a life-style in accordance with this idea, you are one of the oppressors.

The agribusiness corporations which profit by exploiting calves, pigs and chickens don't need your approval; they need your money. The purchase of their products is the only support they seek from the public. As long as they continue to get it, they will have the money and the political muscle to fight off attempts to give animals a decent life. They will be able to say to their critics: 'We are only providing the public with the goods it demands at the price it is prepared to pay'. And they will be able to tell their shareholders that agribusiness is a good investment.

So if you want to stop the practices we have described in the previous chapters of this book, start with yourself. Start by refusing to support practices which abuse animals. This isn't the *only* thing you should do – later in this chapter we'll suggest some others - but it's the place to begin, because it underpins and makes consistent everything else you do for animals. You can't really make an effective show of your regard for animals if you are in the habit of dining on pieces of their flesh. Protesting about bull-fighting in Spain or the slaughter of whales by the Japanese while continuing to eat veal from calves who have been deprived of their mothers, fed on a diet which makes them anaemic, and denied freedom to turn around, is like denouncing apartheid in South Africa while selling the white government arms to keep the blacks in their place.

● Shift to a cruelty-free lifestyle

Becoming a vegetarian isn't a matter of converting to some weird new religion. Just as we would boycott food produced by rulers who enslaved and oppressed their workers, so vegetarianism is simply a boycott of foods produced by those who enslave and oppress animals.

Admittedly, it isn't all *that* simple, because eating animal flesh is a habit which has become deeply entrenched in Western society. The authors of this book know all about this. We too were brought up in families which regarded meat as the centre of every dinner, and most lunches too. On festive occasions, a large dead bird was wheeled in to be carved up as a special treat. So we well understand that the idea of going without meat will still seem shocking to many people who have been brought up in the same way. What else is there to eat?

Fortunately there are plenty of other good things to eat, most of them a lot healthier than flesh anyway. Once you take the first step, you will find that the flesh-eating habit isn't that hard to kick after all. Remember that it is only in Western society that it is considered normal to eat such large quantities of meat every day. In many other cultures, in Japan, China, India, the Pacific Islands and much of Africa, meat is either non-existent, or a rare addition to a diet of grains and vegetables. The unusual good health and long life

118

of some vegetarians, like the Hunzas of Northern India and the people of the Vilcabamba valley in Ecuador, has led many diets designed for health alone, like the famous 'longevity diet' devised by the American Nathan Pritikin, to be virtually free of animal products.

If the idea of doing without meat seems a hardship, it is only because we are unfamiliar with the infinitely varied possibilities of a cuisine which takes all the best in vegetarian cooking from Europe, the Middle East, China, Japan and Mexico, as well as specially created dishes from the new wave of vegetarianism now sweeping the Western world. Once we try these dishes we will find that they bring a new enjoyment of food, based on the knowledge that what we are eating is nourishing, low in fat, free of additives like antibiotics and growth promotants, high in fibre. And above all it has not required the death or suffering of any sentient being.

So what is there to eat? This is not a cookbook, and we aren't about to go into details. There are plenty of excellent vegetarian cookbooks around nowadays and we have listed a few in the back. But meanwhile, here are some ideas to think about:

- Chinese dishes based on stir-fried fresh vegetables served with rice; bean sprouts, nuts or tofu (bean curd) provide the protein.
- Italian cooking offers many possibilities, such as vegetable lasagna, spaghetti with a sauce based on tomatoes, eggplant or other vegetables, and pizza with a variety of toppings.

- There are innumerable Indian dishes: including all sorts of vegetable and potato curries, and also dhal, the popular red lentil curry which is a most inexpensive source of protein.
- Middle Eastern dishes use dried beans in inventive ways – felafel, served in a pouch of pita with lettuce and a tahini sauce, is just one example.
- In many parts of the East – Japan, China, Indonesia and Vietnam, for instance – tofu is a basic part of the popular diet. It is amazing how many tasty dishes can be made with tofu, and there are now entire cookbooks devoted to this high protein, low fat, low calorie food.
- If all of this sounds too exotic for you at this stage, remember that most health food shops sell soya-based meat substitutes which enable you to continue to eat hamburgers and all the other kinds of food you used to eat, without exploiting animals.

Did you notice that these suggestions not only avoid meat, but can also be followed without using other animal products, like eggs, milk and cheese? A diet which avoids *all* animal products is known as a 'vegan' diet. We aren't suggesting that you necessarily go all that way in one step. Start by avoiding the flesh of slaughtered animals, and seeking out eggs from hens who have been able to range freely outside, rather than being locked up in small wire cages. But bear in mind that the dairy industry is based on making cows pregnant, and then removing their calves, so that we humans can have the milk. In the process, both the cows and the calves suffer from the

enforced separation – and many of the calves end up in the veal industry. Moreover in some countries, especially the United States, the dairy industry is following the regrettable example of the poultry and pork industries; cows are being brought indoors and restricted to small stalls which they leave only to be milked.

So when you cut out animal flesh, *don't* make up for it by eating more cheese. Instead, once you have adjusted to doing without meat, think about cutting out dairy products as well. Soyamilk, a product made from soya beans, is similar to milk in taste and nutritional value. It can be obtained from many health food shops, and there are now some soya cheeses. In any case, despite what the dairy industry tries to tell us, milk and cheese are not essential for our health. Many non-Western cuisines use no dairy products, and in fact adults from Africa and Asia are often physically unable to digest milk products. Almonds and sesame seeds are good alternative sources of calcium, as are broccoli and dark green leafy vegetables. Incidentally, eating too much protein – as many meat-eaters do – has been shown to cause calcium loss even in those whose diets are high in calcium.

In fact, you can get every necessary nutrient from plant products, with the possible exception of vitamin B12. This vitamin can be obtained from kelp, or grown from a yeast, and is often contained in nutritional yeast products and in 'B group' vitamin tablets. If you are strict vegan, not eating even eggs from free ranging hens, taking one of these supplements is a good idea, even though many vegans have lived in good health without having done so.

The chances are that a vegetarian or vegan diet will make you healthier than you would otherwise have been. There are now many studies which show that vegetarians and vegans are less likely than meat-eaters to suffer from the two greatest killer diseases of modern society; cancer and heart disease. A vegetarian diet may also help with obesity, diabetes, osteoporosis (which causes brittle bones in old age), kidney stones and diverticulosis, a painful condition of the colon.

122

● Good company, and more of it all the time

You'll be pleased to know that, as a vegetarian, you'll be in good company. Throughout history, many of the most enlightened thinkers have chosen not to eat meat. In the East, an immense number of philosophers, gurus and spiritual leaders have been vegetarian. The tradition starts with the earliest Hindu and Jain leaders, and continues through Buddha and Asoka to Gandhi, Moraji Desai, and the Dalai Lama. In the West, Pythagoras (of the famous theorem) was a vegetarian, and Plato described an ideal community living on a meatless diet in his *Republic*. Some of the most sensitive artists and writers, like Leonardo da Vinci, Percy Shelley, Leo Tolstoy and George Bernard Shaw were vegetarians. More recently outstanding sporting figures have been added to the list: Finnish long distance runner Paavo Nurmi; Australia's Olympic 1500 metre freestyle swimming gold medallist Murray Rose; and US basketball star Bill Walton.

It's also nice to know that several medical studies have shown that vegetarians tend to live longer than other people. Just for interest, after we had compiled the list of famous vegetarians for the preceding paragraph, we decided to check on how long they lived.

We had some trouble with Asoka, the Indian Emperor who died in about 238 BC - his date of birth is not known, and although he appears to have ruled for nearly 40 years, we couldn't establish how old he was when he became emperor. Otherwise, the answers are as follows: Buddha died at 80; Gandhi was 79 when he was shot by an assassin; Moraji Desai was Prime Minister of India at the age of 84, and is now 90; Pythagoras is believed to have lived to 75 (when he was murdered) and Plato to 80 (although there is no evidence that Plato was a vegetarian, apart from his advocacy of such a diet); Leonardo da Vinci lived 67 years, and Shelley only 30 (but since he was drowned while sailing he doesn't count); Tolstoy lived to 82, and Shaw to 94. The Dalai Lama and the sporting figures mentioned are all still alive and relatively young.

LEONARDO

SHAW

TOLSTOY

GANDHI

125

These results surprised even us. Taking into account the shorter average lifespan of earlier times, it is remarkable that (putting aside the unfortunate Shelley) all except Leonardo passed the traditional 'three score and ten', and a majority lived to eighty or beyond, well above even today's average male life-expectancy.

In the last ten years, as more and more people have come to understand both the ethical and health reasons for becoming vegetarian, the swing to a meatless diet has gathered pace. In the United States there are now six million vegetarians; in Britain, 1.5 million. The number is growing by 30% each year, a rate which has caused real alarm among meat producers.

● Flex your consumer muscles

Animal exploitation is all around us. An incredible number of ordinary products on the market are, in some way or another, the result of animal slaughter. But it doesn't have to be this way. The exploitation will continue only as long as it is profitable.

As consumers, we can change this. In addition to giving up animal foods and using canvas and synthetics in place of furs and leather, we can boycott products that contain dead animals or that have been tested on animals. Did you know that civet, an ingredient in expensive perfumes, is scraped from the glands of Ethiopian civet cats, who have been kept in tiny bamboo cages and subjected to heat and smoke in order to make the glands secrete more? Musk, another perfume fixative, is obtained by killing the small Himalayan musk deer. And if perfumes and cosmetics do not contain such ingredients, they are still very likely to have been tested on animals in painful ways.

In order to avoid causing needless animal suffering each of us can refrain from buying 'new and improved' products and instead stay with those made from long-used ingredients. Better still, we can avoid products manufactured by companies whose policies involve the suffering and death of 'civet ... is scraped from the glands of Ethiopian civet cats who have been kept in tiny bamboo cages and subjected to heat and smoke ... Musk ... is obtained by killing the small Himalayan musk deer.'

millions of innocent animals. Colgate-Palmolive, Bristol-Myers, Gillette, Johnson and Johnson, and many others produce cosmetics and household products which contain animals or have been tested on animals. In contrast several companies have been set up specifically to produce cosmetics which are guaranteed cruelty-free. (They use natural ingredients which have been widely and safely used for a long time). In most countries there are other companies which make the same promise; find out which they are, and buy their products. (Some of them are listed in the back of this book). The choice is ours.

Voting against cruelty by putting our money into safe, effective non-animal products is one very important way to minimise animal suffering in our daily lives. By letting the big animal exploiters know we will not use their products until they stop harming animals we can eventually change this crude practice on a grand scale. Write letters, make phone calls and let your local supermarkets know that you are boycotting these products and why. Ask shops in your area to start carrying 'cruelty-free' products and put up displays to inform customers. As demand shifts away from animal cruelty, the market will respond.

In all of this, you should try to be as consistent as you can, but you don't have to get carried away with a desire to be fanatically pure. The object is to deny your money to industries based on animal exploitation. It isn't worth spending all day looking for a cruelty-free toothpaste – if it is that difficult to get, it would have been more effective to use your time working with an animal rights group on one of their campaigns.

Which brings us to the other things you should be doing.

● Spread the word

You will have greater impact if you encourage others to join you. Let your family, business associates, friends, neighbours, and everyone you can tell, know how animals are exploited all around them. Learn more about the animal liberation issue by reading and then pass the books on to

130

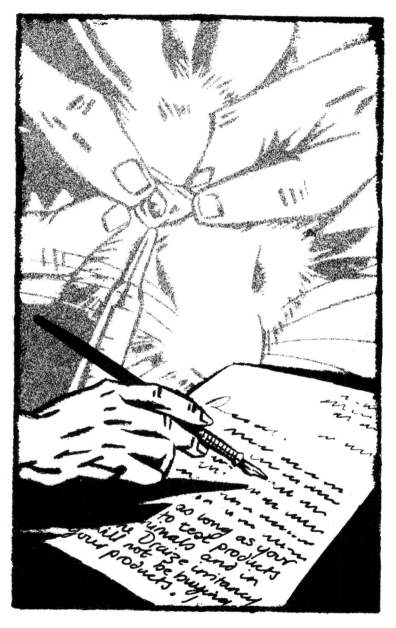

131

others. The more you know, the easier it will be to convey your message.

You can spread the word by making flyers, posters, and leaflets and posting them around town. Visit your local schools and schedule a speaker or show on the animal issue. Set up information booths at shopping centres. Find out when travelling fairs and shows will be in your area and set up displays. Donate books on animal liberation to your local library and while you are there make arrangements to set up a display table or bulletin board.

Ask your favourite newspapers and magazines to write or publish an article on animal rights. Write letters to the editor. Learn how to produce free public service announcements for television and radio. Take advantage of public access stations.

If you are a student, a teacher, or have any connection with a school where students are required to dissect animals, start campaigning for an end to such an uncivilised practice. Dissection teaches that life is cheap and it makes otherwise compassionate people less sensitive to the value of animal life. Students can learn biology without having to cut up animals. There are many alternatives available, including films, models and computer programs. Seek them out, and help promote students' rights to a non-violent education.

Link up with other people who are interested in the animal issue. If there is no animal rights group in your area, start one. (It's really amazing how often people with no previous experience or qualifications have been able to start off groups which have made a huge impact and spared thousands of animals from suffering and death). Contact national animal rights groups for information and advice.

Most people are unaware of the cruelty involved in everyday living. Once they become informed, compassionate people will opt for a non-exploitative lifestyle, especially when they realise that it does not require much effort and that they are not alone.

● Campaign for animal rights

Successful campaigns require thoughtful planning, thorough research, and a wide variety of action. Whether it's a national or a local campaign, the most important element is commitment. It is vital for the whole movement that animal advocates are not seen as people who will get tired, bored, or distracted from this particular issue and will move on to something else. Campaigners must always be well organised and ready to surprise their opponents with their ingenuity and persistence.

● Do your homework

Any campaign requires hours of thorough research. For the most part, the suffering that occurs on factory farms, the cruelty involved in the fur industry, and the exploitation of animals in entertainment is well documented and accessible. Major libraries and established animal rights organisations are a good place to start gathering information.

Documentation on animal experimentation requires more independent digging at the outset since what goes on in one laboratory differs from what goes on in another. The best place to begin is a university or medical library. Find out the names of animal experimenters by looking in university catalogues. You can bet that the person teaching 'Experimental Psychology' or 'Methods of Toxicology' also experiments on animals. Once you discover who the animal experimenters are, you can look up their published articles to find out what kinds of experiments they are doing. Despite the fact that these articles are written by the experimenters themselves, the experiments are almost always graphically described.

In countries which have a Freedom of Information Act, such as the US and Australia, gaining information is really quite simple. The act must be used with care however, because FOI requests can tip-off potential targets. In the US, a federal agency that releases any information must inform the target that inquiries are being made, and by whom. So it is advisable to do as much preliminary information gathering as possible before making any requests.

Researching animal cruelty is a form of detective work. Every source of information, no matter how unlikely or bizarre, may be useful – peruse old newspapers, contact business and professional monitoring agencies, check public records, work undercover, and never stop asking questions. If you happen upon someone who works inside a facility which uses animals, try to develop the contact. Inside information is invaluable. But make sure everything that you say is 100% accurate and can be documented. In every public statement you make, the credibility of the animal liberation movement will be at stake.

• Choose your target carefully

When choosing a target it is crucial to be selective. Military weapons or radiation testing, psychology experiments involving obvious pain (like electric shock) or distress (like isolation for a normally social animal) and toxicity testing of cosmetics or other non-medical products are good choices because they can easily be seen to be both painful and unnecessary. Obviously frivolous practices, such as selling fur coats or promoting veal, are also good targets.

In many cases, you may not be as free to choose a target because an obvious opportunity may present itself. This was the case with a University of Florida experiment. A newspaper reporter uncovered a proposal to drown 42 dogs in order to test something known as 'the Heimlich manoeuvre'. Dr Heimlich himself, after whom the manoeuvre was named, had strenuously objected to this cruel proposal which was being considered for funding by the American Heart Association. In this instance, the activists had to choose not what type of abuse to target, but whom. In the end activists in Florida attacked the University while others in Washington, DC confronted the American Heart Association. As a result the proposal was withdrawn and the plans for the experiment cancelled.

Before any campaign is put in action, activists must take into account not only how objectionable the animal abuse is, but also how it appears to the public. You must determine how

136

vulnerable the target is to public pressure, how much power or influence the target has in the community, and the public perception of the target facility.

• Set attainable goals

When planning action, always ask 'What can we realistically achieve?' The goals you set must be reasonable. If you are asking too much, the public may see you as fanatics. If your goals are reasonable and are presented in such a way as to provide benefits to both humans and non-humans, then your opponents look unreasonable when they resist your efforts. In all campaigns, it is important to remain true to the ultimate goal – animal liberation. Compromising too soon will not only ruin your credibility but will not help the animals. But this doesn't mean that you should aim at ending all animal abuse at a single stroke. Victories along the way are stepping stones to the ultimate goal. They also help individual animals who cannot wait for the final triumph.

• Vary your tactics

After the groundwork has been laid, and you have decided it is time to go public, contact your target and present your complaints. Ask for a meeting to discuss the problems and possible solutions. Most likely your requests will be denied, but it is worth the attempt because your opponent will not have the opportunity to say 'They never discussed any problems with us'. Besides, you have nothing to lose if you are well prepared, and who knows, you just may get what you want for the animals.

Contacting organisations and individuals who support your target can be a very effective tactic. For example, activists who were protesting against sex experiments on cats at the American Museum of Natural History generated so much mail that the then-Congressman Ed Koch insisted on visiting the Museum to inspect the facilities. Hundreds of museum supporters cancelled their memberships, and at least one would-be-benefactor cut the museum out of her will.

After beginning by contemptuously dismissing the protests, the Museum had to bow to the pressure in the end.

... So I said to the doctor who was explaining what was happening: 'What do you do here? What is the purpose of this experiment?' And she said, 'Well, the purpose is to look at the effect of hyper – and hypo-sexuality in cats. We find,' said she, 'that if you take a normal male cat and you place that cat in a room with a female cat that is in heat, the male cat would mount the female cat.'

I said, 'That sounds very reasonable to me.'

Then she said, 'Now if you take a cat, a male cat, and you put lesions in its brain –'

I interrupted and asked, 'What are lesions?'

She said, 'Well, you destroy part of the brain cells.'

I asked, 'What happens then?'

She said, 'Well, if you take that male cat that has lesions in its brain and you place it in a room with a female cat and a female rabbit, the cat will mount the rabbit.'

I said to her, 'How does that rabbit feel about all this?'

There was no response.

Then I said to this professor, 'Now, tell me, after you have taken a deranged male cat with brain lesions and you place it in a room and you find that it is going to mount a rabbit instead of a female cat, what have you got?'

There was no response.

... I said, 'How much has this cost the government?'

She said, '$435,000.'

(from Ed Koch's report in the 'Congressional Record')

Political lobbying is another effective tool for change. Contact your elected representative by letter, follow up with a telephone call and set up an appointment. Let them know specifically what your concerns are and what you would like them to do about it. Politicians respond to reason, thorough documentation, and political pressure. Bring statements from experts condemning the practice you are protesting. Bring in letters or petitions signed by others who share your concern. Show the politicians that the animal abuse you are opposing is wasteful and frivolous.

By getting the media involved in your campaign, you can reach millions of people. Stage a newsworthy event and notify the press. Plan a demonstration at a site which is meaningful to the campaign, invite prominent speakers and activists, use props, costumes, and other theatrical devices. Choose spokespeople who are well-presented and articulate. Have information packs and a prepared statement ready for the press.

139

At a successful demonstration in front of the US Department of Agriculture, activists gathered to protest against a new law which would require that dairy farmers brand their cows in the face before selling them for slaughter. One protester, dressed as the grim reaper, wielded a mock branding iron which marked the demonstrators' faces with an X. The press covered the event and the news went out to the nation.

● Direct action

Often the most effective way to end a particularly abusive practice is to intervene directly on behalf of the animals. The intervention can range from independent spontaneous events to carefully planned group actions. Direct action can involve breaking the law, so activists must be prepared to pay the price, which may mean spending some time in jail. This, after all, is in the best tradition of non-violent civil disobedience as a way of opposing something that is morally wrong – the method developed by Gandhi and Martin Luther King.

In England, a group of committed activists decided to sabotage a circus which was coming to their town. They put 'cancelled' stickers across the posters advertising the circus. They even placed an advertisement in the local paper advising that the circus had been cancelled. When the circus arrived, only 30 people turned up, causing the promoters to lose heavily. Other British animal rights campaigners have spray-painted or dyed furs in stores, and put superglue in their doorlocks.

In these cases, the animal campaigners felt that to continue to be effective, they had to remain anonymous. In others, such as disrupting conventions held by animal exploiters, or blocking the entrance to fur stores, activists cannot be anonymous and are likely to be arrested. In these instances, it is advisable to have a lawyer on hand, and money available to pay bail. In dealing with police and the courts, remember that the authorities are not necessarily opposed to the cause of animal liberation; they are just doing their duty by enforcing the law.

In planning direct action, though, it is vital to look beyond the immediate target of your activity to the future of the animal liberation movement as a whole. A single raid may save fifty, or a hundred, or even a thousand animals; but the aim of the movement is to save *billions* of animals every year. We can only make progress towards this goal if we convince the public that our cause is right. This can be achieved if we show, in our deeds as well as in our words, the greatest

142

possible compassion for *all* animals, the human ones along with the non-human.

There are many things that can and should be done to expose animal exploitation. We have mentioned only a few. Whether you decide to become a vegetarian, write letters, picket the local fur shop, block the entrance to a slaughter house, enter a lab to photograph animal abuse, or do all of these and more, the steps you take, in your own home or your community, are steps that matter. The struggle for animal liberation will undoubtedly be a long one. But every individual action brings the animals closer to the day when they will no longer be treated as mere things for humans to use at will.

143

Human animals tend to resist change. It usually takes more than quiet rumblings to end cruel and even barbaric practices. The sooner you decide to voice your objections to speciesism, the sooner we will achieve a more just world for all beings – human and non-human alike.

Further Reading

General

Godlovitch, Stanley and Roslind, and Harris, John, *Animals, Men and Morals*, London, Gollancz, 1972. A path-breaking collection of articles.

Midgley, Mary, *Animals and Why They Matter*, Harmondsworth, Penguin, 1984. A penetrating discussion of the difference that species makes.

Regan, Tom, *The Case For Animal Rights*, Berkeley, University of California Press, 1984. The fullest elaboration of the philosophical arguments for attributing rights to animals.

Regan, Tom and Singer, Peter (eds) *Animal Rights and Human Obligations*, Englewood Cliffs, N.J., Prentice-Hall, 1976. An anthology of writings, from both sides, on the animal issue.

Salt, Henry, *Animal Rights*, Fontwell, Sussex, Centaur Press, 1980 (first published 1892). An early classic.

Singer, Peter, *Animal Liberation*, New York. A New York Review Book, 1975; Avon, 1977; Wellingborough, Thorsons, 1983. A new ethic for our treatment of animals.

Singer, Peter (ed) *In Defence of Animals,* Oxford, Blackwell, 1985. A collection of writings by leading activists and thinkers.

Turner, E.S. *All Heaven in a Rage*, London, Michael Joseph, 1964. An informative and entertaining history of the movement for animal protection.

Wynne-Tyson, J. (ed) *The Extended Circle: A Dictionary of Humane Thought*, Fontwell, Sussex, Centaur Press, 1985.

Animals in Research

Rowan, Andrew, *Of Mice, Models and Men; A Critical Evaluation of Animal Research*, Albany, State University of New York Press, 1984. An up-to-date examination by a scientist.

Ryder, Richard, *Victims of Science*, London, Davis-Poynter, 1975; National Anti-Vivisection Society, 1983. Still the best overall account of animal experimentation.

Behind the Laboratory Door, The Animal Welfare Institute, Washington, DC, 1985. A carefully researched look at American laboratories.

Kotzwinkle, William, *Dr Rat*, New York, Knopf, 1976. A witty novel written from the perspective of an experimental rat.

Farm Animals and the Meat Industry

Agriculture Committee, House of Commons, *Animal Welfare in Poultry, Pig and Veal Calf Production*, London, HMSO., 1981. An authoritative government report which comes out firmly against many current practices.

Brambell, F.W.R., (Chairman), *Report of the Technical Committee to Enquire into the Welfare of Animals kept under Intensive Livestock Husbandry Systems*, London, HMSO., 1965. The report of the first detailed government enquiry into factory farming.

Gold, Mark, *Assault and Battery*, London, Pluto Press, 1983. An examination of factory farming.

Harrison, Ruth, *Animal Machines*, London, Vincent Stuart, 1964. The book that started the campaign against factory farming.

Lappe, Francis More, *Diet for a Small Planet*, New York, Ballantine, 1971. This book argues on ecological grounds against meat production.

Mason, Jim and Singer, Peter, *Animal Factories*, New York, Crown, 1980. The health, ecological and animal welfare implications of factory farming, with an outstanding collection of photographs.

148

Vegetarianism

Akers, Keith, *A Vegetarian Sourcebook*, New York, Putnam, 1983. The most comprehensive collection of up-to-date scientific information on the vegetarian diet.

Braunstein, Mark, *Radical Vegetarianism*, Los Angeles, Pajandrum, 1981. On the nutritional and ethical aspects of vegetarianism.

Kapleau, Philip, *To Cherish All Life*, Rochester, N.Y., The Zen Centre, 1981. A Buddhist view of animal slaughter and meat eating, by an eminent American Buddhist.

Wynne-Tyson, John, *Food For a Future*, London, Sphere, 1976. An argument for vegetarianism on humane and ecological grounds.

Wildlife

Amory, Cleveland, *Mankind?*, New York, Dell, 1980. A scathing critique of the war on wildlife.

Batten, Peter, *Living Trophies*, New York, Crowell, 1976. A critical look at zoos and what they do to animals.

Baker, Ron, *The American Hunting Myth*, New York, Vantage Press, 1985. A well-researched indictment of killing for fun.

Day, David, *The Doomsday Book of Animals*, New York, Viking Press, 1980. How we are driving numerous species to extinction.

Cookbooks

There are thousands of vegetarian and vegan cookbooks on the market. Here are just a few highly recommended ones.

Hagler, L., *Tofu Cookery*, The Book Publishing Company, Tennessee, 1982.

Hagler, L., *The Farm Vegetarian Cookbook*, The Book Publishing Company, Tennessee, 1979.

Robertson, L., et.al, *The New Laurel's Kitchen*, Tenspeed Press, Berkeley, 1986.

Useful Organisations

Here are just a few of the most active and effective organisations. The fact that an organisation is not listed here should not be taken to mean that it is not useful – it may be, or it may not be.

Australia and New Zealand

Animal Liberation – State offices are as follows:
Canberra, PO Box 1875, ACT 2601.
New South Wales, 20 Enmore Rd., Newtown, NSW 2402.
Northern Territory, PO Box 49277 Casuarina, NT 5792.
Queensland, GPO Box 1787, Brisbane, Qld. 4001.
South Australia, 118 Hutt St., Adelaide, SA 5000.
Tasmania, 102 Bathurst St., Hobart, Tas. 7000.
Victoria, GPO Box 1196 K, Melbourne, Vic. 3001.
Western Australia, PO Box 146 Inglewood, WA 6052.

Animal Liberation – The Magazine
PO Box 15, Elwood,
Vic. 3184.

For further details of organisations in Australia and New Zealand, contact the Australian and New Zealand Federation of Animal Societies, PO Box 200, Greensborough, Vic. 3088.

Canada

ARK II – Canadian Animal Rights Network
542 Mt. Pleasant Road #104,
Toronto, Ontario M4S 2M7.

Lifeforce
PO Box 3117,
Main Post Office,
Vancouver, B.C. V6B 3X6.

Germany

Mobilisation fuer Tiers e. V.,
Postfach 977, 3400 Goettingen.

Netherlands

Nederlandse Bond tot Bestrijding van de Vivisectie,
Jan van Nassaustraat 81,
2596 BR's-Gravenhage.

Sweden

Nordiska Samfundet Mot Plagsamma Djurforsok,
Drottninggatan 102,
11160 Stockholm.

United Kingdom

Animal Aid,
7 Castle Street,
Tonbridge, Kent, TN9 1BH.

British Union for the Abolition of Vivisection,
16a Crane Grove,
Islington, London N7 8LB.

Compassion in World Farming,
20 Lavant Street,
Petersfield,
Hampshire.

The Scottish Anti-Vivisection Society,
121 West Regent Street,
Glasgow, G2 2SD.

Vegan Society,
33 - 35 George Street,
Oxford, OX1 2AY.

Vegetarian Society,
Parkdale,
Dunham Road,
Altrincham,
Cheshire.

USA

The Animals' Agenda,
PO Box 5234,
Westport, CT 06881.

The Animal Legal Defense Fund,
333 Market Street Suite 2300,
San Francisco, CA 94105.

Farm Animal Reform Movement,
PO Box 70123,
Washington, DC 20088.

The Fund for Animals.
200 W. 57th Street,
New York, NY 10019.

The International Primate Protection League,
PO Box 766,
Summerville, SC 29484.

**The International Society For Animal Rights,
421 South State Street,
Clarks Summit,
Pennsylvania 18411.**

National Alliance for Animal Legislation,
PO Box 77012,
Washington, DC 20013.

The National Anti-Vivisection Society,
10 East Ohio Street,
Chicago, Illinois 60611.

People for the Ethical Treatment of Animals,
PO Box 42516,
Washington, DC 20015.

Student Action Corps For Animals,
PO Box 15588,
Washington, DC 20003.

Trans-Species,
PO Box 1553,
Williamsport,
Pennsylvania 17703.

Cruelty-Free Products

All of the following will send catalogues so that you can order by mail.

Australia

Beauty Without Cruelty,
PO Box 93,
North Melbourne, Vic. 3051,
or
GPO Box 1787,
Brisbane, Qld. 4001.

United Kingdom

Beauty Without Cruelty,
37 Avebury Avenue,
Tonbridge,
Kent.

The Body Shop International
Dominion Way,
Rustington,
W. Sussex.

Honesty Cosmetics,
33 Markham Road Chesterfield, Derbyshire.

Naturally Yours Cosmetics,
Freepost, 7 Tudor Road,
Broadheath, Altrincham, Cheshire.

United States

Amberwood,
Route 1, Box 206,
Milner, GA 30257.

Vegan Street,
P.O. Box 5525,
Rockville, MD 20855.

My Brothers' Keeper
P.O. Box 1769,
Richmond, IN 47375.

Paul Penders,
D & P Products,
P.O. Box 878,
Old Canning Plant Rd.,
Seffner, FL 33584.

Direct Action Groups

The Animal Liberation Front,
BCM Box 1160,
London WC1N 3XX.

The ALF Support Group (UK),
BCM Box 1160,
London WC1N 3XX.

The ALF Support Group– Canada,
PO Box 915,
Station F,
Toronto, Ontario M4Y 2N9.

Direct Action for Animal Rights,
PO Box 152,
Lutwyche, Queensland, Australia.

Hunt Saboteurs Association,
PO Box 87,
Exeter EX4 3TX.

Lomakatsi,
Box 1315,
1900 M Street NW
Washington DC 2003.

Northern Animal Liberation League,
PO Box 96,
Manchester M60 4AL.
England

GRAPHIC GUIDES
Series editor: Philip Boys

Anarchy
Clifford Harper

Animal Liberation
Lori Gruen, Peter Singer & David Hine

Apartheid
Donald Woods & Mike Bostock

Media and Power
Peter Lewis & Corinne Pearlman

Modern Art
Dave Clarke & Julie Hollings

Space Wars
Martin Ince & David Hine

Thatcher
Ed Harriman & John Freeman

Women Artists
Frances Borzello & Natacha Ledwidge

Forthcoming titles

The Birth of the Woman's Novel
Dale Spender & Natacha Ledwidge

Language and Power
Rob Pope & Graham Higgins

Logic and Power
Herb Kohl & Robin Collingwood

Radiation and Health
Tony Webb & Robin Collingwood

Revolutionary Women
Cathy Porter & Anna Louise